We JOURNEY with Christ

Lenten and Easter Meditations

VELMA RUCH
Editor

Herald Publishing House, Independence 64051

Printed in the United States of America

11 10 09 08 07 06 5 4 3 2 1

Library of Congress Cataloging-in-Publication Data

We journey with Christ: Lenten and Easter meditations/Velma Ruch, editor.
p. cm.
ISBN-13: 978-0-8309-1227-8
ISBN-10: 0-8309-1227-4
1. Lent--Meditations. 2. Easter--Meditations. I. Ruch, Velma.
BV85.W38 2006
242'.34--dc22
2006000725

ISBN-10 0-8309-1227-4
ISBN-13 978-0-8309-1227-8

The publisher gratefully acknowledges permission to quote from the following publications.

Acknowledgments

All of us, regardless of denomination, are blessed with a treasure of thoughtful and creative writing contributed by Christian scholars dedicated to spiritual formation.and a deeper understanding of Christian discipleship. In assembling the materials for these meditations I searched once again through books and periodicals that had become precious to me to sort out and share with the readers of this volume the heart of some of these writings. The authors whose works are cited here are too many to mention, but they are listed in the body of the work as well as in the bibliography. I wish to express particular appreciation for Wendy J. Miller's book, *Jesus Our Spiritual Director,* for her insights into the life of Jesus and for giving me the basis for the organization of these meditations. Wendy M. Wright's three books centered in the Church Year: *The Vigil: Keeping Watch in the Season of Christ's Coming; The Rising: Living the Mysteries of Lent, Easter, and Pentecost;* and *The Time Between: Cycles and Rhythms In Ordinary Time,* have been my constant companions as I have attempted to go deeper in my understanding of the Christian Year. As I have sorted through my own writings to find material that might be worth saying once again I was struck by the many, both living and dead, who have deeply influenced me and whose words speak through my own. The Scriptures, which form the core of this material, are supreme among these. I have used the three books sacred to the Community of Christ: The Bible, The Book of Mormon, and The Doctrine and Covenants. It is my prayer that you will find renewed appreciation for these volumes as you open yourself to their spiritual wisdom once again.

I wish to express special appreciation to Scott Murphy, president of the Lamoni Heartland Mission Center for appointing and supporting a spiritual formation committee; for Dick Young who chaired that committee, and for the individual members whose thoughts spurred me to these writings. Special appreciation goes to Rich Brown and his associates at Herald House who accepted this work for publication and asked me to write two additional volumes. When under the pressure of church finance, publication was put on hold, many offered to pay for publication costs if Graceland University's Media Center could assist in preparing the material for publication. That came to pass under the leadership of Dennis Piepergerdes and his dedicated staff. Special appreciation goes to Steve Edwards who designed the cover and planned the layout. Church leaders and Herald House staff are overseeing the publication and distribution of the material.. My deep gratitude goes to them all and to the many unnamed who have given their time and effort to this project.

CONTENTS

WE JOURNEY WITH CHRIST
LENTEN AND EASTER MEDITATIONS

INTRODUCTION

In the opening sentence of his book *Addiction and Grace,* Gerald May stated, "After twenty years of listening to the yearnings of people's hearts, I am convinced that all human beings have an inborn desire for God." Dr. May went on to say that "whether we are consciously religious or not, this desire is our deepest longing, and our most precious treasure....Regardless of how we describe it, it is a longing for love. It is a hunger to love, to be loved, and to move closer to the source of love." The longing is God-induced and can only truly be satisfied through a growing intimacy with its source. The scriptures and meditations assembled in this small volume have been compiled and designed to assist us in that process. Many voices speak to us through these readings and help us see an old story, but an eternally living story, with new eyes. We share in the writer's vision and are encouraged to join in the journey to abundant life.

The inspiration for these Lenten meditations had their origin in the Spiritual Formation Committee appointed by Scott Murphy, president of the Lamoni Heartland Mission Center In creating the committee Brother Murphy stated,

> "It is my hope that we can begin to assist people (as leaven or advocates) in experiencing, in a conscious and intentional way, a deeper spiritual relationship with God. There is a need to provide opportunities for people to encounter a 'healing of their spirit' that frees them and empowers them in the journey toward an abundant life. For me, this can only be through a profound relationship with God. I see this team as offering leadership that will result in a variety of different experiences and mediums to engage people in the use of spiritual practices, and ending ultimately in their formation in God. We should invite people on a journey – a journey that evolves over time and offers a spiritual vitality to individual lives and the life of the church."

The committee under the leadership of Dick Young has explored over a number of months how to assist in accomplishing this. Among our various proposals came a suggestion that one way we might alert our people to the whole process of spiritual formation was to engage them in scriptures and meditations related to the church year.

Because of timing we decided to begin with Lent. It fell to my lot to contribute to this effort by doing the necessary writing and collection of materials. After some initial frustration on my part the project took fire in me and I experienced what the disciples on the road to Emmaus referred to as "the burning heart." I was indeed experiencing again a story I thought I already knew by heart. I awoke each day with a desire to get on with it, to read more, to think more, to write more. I was in some respects overwhelmed by the wealth of material at my disposal to the point that I found selection difficult and the result was more material than either I or the committee had originally envisioned. Publication has become possible through the cooperation of the Graceland University Media Center and Herald House. In the publication we hope to reach beyond our intention to work with our own mission center and minister to a wider public in the church and beyond. It is the plan that this booklet will be followed by two others: *Transformation: The Journey from Easter to Pentecost,* and *Finding Home: Advent, Christmas, and Epiphany.* Though the church year traditionally begins with Advent, since we began the process with Lent, we'll continue from there and end with the Advent sequence. At what point we begin does not matter so much as our willingness to enter the journey to live more fully in God's presence.

We invite persons to participate in these readings in ways appropriate to their needs and the time available to them for daily devotions. To seriously relate to both the scriptures and meditations included under each day would be more time consuming than many can afford and would not necessarily be helpful. Attempting to rush through or worrying about "not doing it right" would defeat the purpose. Each day we have the opportunity to choose the part or parts that meet our need that day and we should allow ourselves to focus on that aspect. It may even come down to just a phrase that will take root in our minds and stay with us throughout the day. There will always be opportunity to come back as time allows and to meditate further on those parts that may yet be open to our prepared spirits. Each day is likely to be different. In the process we may discover a multitude of different ways to live in the Spirit. To recognize the way or ways that are most meaningful to our personal temperament at any given time is part of the delight of spiritual formation. That will vary as we grow in "power and light" and will always be under the guidance of the Spirit. In coming to each day's readings we place ourselves before God and we should take time to prayerfully clear our minds, to make room for the Spirit's presence. Our task is to come, to be prepared and ready to receive. What happens next is beyond our control. Though to our perception we may have "good days" and "bad days," as long as we stay on the road we allow the Spirit to work its miracles in us. "Our competence," as the Apostle Paul once stated it so eloquently, "is from God, who has made us competent to be ministers of a new covenant, not of letter but of spirit; for the letter kills, but the Spirit gives life (2 Cor. 3:4). Little by little we are transformed into the image of Jesus Christ. In these readings the life, death and resurrection of the Word that became flesh is constantly before our eyes. May we through them be led on the journey to the abundant life.

Velma Ruch

LENTEN REFLECTIONS — Henri J. M. Nouwen

Lent is the most important time of the year to nurture our inner life. It is the time during which we not only prepare ourselves to celebrate the mystery of the death and resurrection of Jesus, but also the death and resurrection that constantly takes place within us. Life is a continuing process of the death of the old and the familiar, and being reborn again into a new hope, a new trust, and a new love. The death and resurrection of Jesus therefore is not just an historical event that took place a long time ago, but an inner event that takes place in our own heart when we are willing to be attentive to it. True repentance is an interior attitude in which we are willing to let go of everything that prevents us from growing into spiritual maturity, and there is hardly a moment in our lives in which we are not invited to detach ourselves from certain ways of thinking, ways of speaking, ways of acting, that for a long time gave us energy, but that always again need to be renewed and recreated.

Lent offers a beautiful opportunity to discover the mystery of Christ within us. It is a gentle but also demanding time. It is a time of solitude but also community. It is a time of listening to the voice within, but also a time of paying attention to other people's needs.

It is a time to continuously make the passage to new inner life as well as to life with those around us.

When we live Lent attentively and gently, then Easter can truly be a celebration during which the full proclamation of the risen Christ will reverberate into the deepest place of our being.

(*Introduction to booklet, Called to Life, Called to Love* composed of reflections selected from Bread for Life by Henri Nouwen, 1996. Published by Creative Communications for the Parish, 1997).

LIFE AS A JOURNEY

Everett Graffeo

We are Voyagers by God's Design. We are on a journey. We cross deserts, we find oases, traverse valleys, climb mountains. We walk on smooth paths, rough, rocky roads that are wide, narrow, long or short; sometimes we take the high road, other times the low road.

Life is so much of a journey. We have a beginning called birth; we have an ending called death. The journey is a life time. We believe there is a destination toward which we move. We experience crowds and long lonely desert stretches. We choose wrong turns, we get off the trail, and we get poison ivy. We wander in the darkness, we fall and break a leg. We climb the mountains, we see the possibilities beyond the distant horizon. We return to the valleys, and walk through flowered fields and cross raging rivers. We make our way, the best we know how – laughing and dancing or sobbing and groping, burdened with the struggle or light-hearted with the opportunity, creative and hoping, or destructive and despairing.

It is not where we journey, or what we do on the journey; the most important thing is who we meet on the journey and how we share with those we meet. Jesus, the

scriptures say, chose 12 that they might be with him. This is at the heart of the meaning of companions. He chose 12 that they might companion him on his journey. They left everything – home, occupation, friends and neighbors, village community, security – to be with him; to be companions for three years. They grew in their experience together. They had struggles, joys of the crowds, sharing meals together, sitting at his feet on the hillside listening to his teachings, the confrontations with the religious leaders, meeting the daily needs of life together.

The companionship experienced by Jesus and his disciples came to culmination at the Passover – Judas Iscariot was no longer there with them. He said to them, "I no longer call you servants, but call you friends." – the companionship they had experienced the last three years had become a deeply loving and trusted relationship. They were friends.

Is it any wonder that when Jesus told them that he must go away and that where he went they could not come it was an agonizing moment for these newly named friends. Their hearts were grieved by his words to them. They become anxious. The companion- ship had been so enriching to their lives. They had changed so much over the three years of intimate association with Jesus. They didn't want to go back to the old way of life.

He said, "*I must go away and I will send unto you another Counselor – the Holy Spirit. The Spirit will be your companion and if I do not go away the Counselor will not come to you. He will guide you into all truth.*" Later he says, "*I am with you always even until the end of the age*" He was giving them a promise that he would be their companion through the presence of the Holy Spirit. He was asking them to believe and to trust his words to them.

In confirmation we are alerted to the fact that the Spirit promised by Jesus to his disciples is the same Spirit who is our companion on our journey. What God wants to have happen is that this acquaintance and realization of the presence of the Spirit will become a deep and abiding friendship. May it be so as we each continue our journeys.

SPIRITUALITY

Everett Graffeo

My personal definition of Spirituality is **living life in the Spirit**. If God is love, then the Spirit of God is love. Spirituality is living the life of love. Paul's letter to the Corinthians addresses spirituality in the well-known thirteenth chapter:

> *If I speak in the tongues of men and of angels, but have not love, I am only a resounding gong or a clanging cymbal. If I have the gift of prophecy and can fathom all mysteries and all knowledge, and if I have a faith that can move mountains, but have not love, I am nothing. If I give all I possess to the poor and surrender my body to the flames, but have not love, I gain nothing.*

The beginning of our inward journey in discovering our spirituality is at the time when we finally realize our spirituality is not our own creation. Our spirituality is not of our own making. Spirituality is not the personal pursuit of an individual to heal the self through certain spiritual disciplines. This reduces spirituality to nothing more than an exercise in self-satisfaction and self-gratification of a sense of personal fulfillment and self-betterment.

Our spirituality is designed by God in our very being at birth. It is the presence of his love, and it is what God continues to do in us throughout our lives, through the nurturing presence of this divine love.

As God is spiritual, so are we spiritual. As God is love, so are we to be love. God sent his Son because of his nature which is love. God's Son is God's love embodied. Authentic spirituality works to the end of opening us to Truth – Jesus Christ – who is "the Way, the Truth, and the Life." Truth is not a principle that works but an incarnation that lives, confronts us, and calls us. Spirituality calls us to Paul's image where "we see face to face." The image is one of mutuality – we see that we are so similar – and the image speaks back to us and says, "You are accountable for others in the world." It is love that truly transforms our lives. Our deepest source of knowledge and understanding is love. Love transforms our way of "knowing" and "being." Truth draws us into personal responsiveness and accountability to the world of which we are a part.

We could call this mutual indwelling. Our spirituality is discovered when we discern Christ in our own lives, and in that of our brothers and sisters. We come full circle in our spirituality when we recognize that we are in Christ. Jesus said, *"I am in you and you are in me." –"Abide in me and I will abide in you."*

Spirituality involves us in learning how to live with imperfection, to live with the paradoxes of life. We are filled with self-deception. Spirituality engages us in facing ourselves squarely and honestly, being able to see ourselves as mixed up, paradoxical and incomplete, imperfect human beings. Spirituality leads us to admit to our powerlessness, to our lack of answers, and to accept the fact that we are not in control. God is.

FORMATIONAL READING

Velma Ruch

For these Lenten meditations we are inviting you to individual transformation through praying the scripture, a method known as formational reading. Thomas Merton in *Opening the Bible* says that the reading of scripture requires "two levels of under-standing: first, a preliminary unraveling of the texts themselves ...which is mainly a matter of knowledge acquired by study; then a deeper level, a living insight which grows out of personal knowledge and relatedness. Only on this second level is the Bible really grasped."

The first level is really only preparation and is not an end in itself. It is only as we see the first level as preparatory to the second, our personal involvement, that we are truly learning to read scripture effectively. Every Christian bookstore is likely to have books dealing with praying the scripture, or formative reading. One of the best books on the subject that I know is M. Robert Mulholland Jr., *Shaped by the Word: The Power of Scripture in Spiritual Formation.* He sees scripture as standing close to the center of the whole process of becoming conformed to the image of Christ. Because scripture is "one of the focal means whereby God awakens us to the dynamics and possibilities of a new way of being," Mulholland contends, "It is important that we learn to approach scripture in a way that can allow it to become a transforming encounter with God."

Formational reading is not an attempt to cover as much material as possible. Rather, it is focusing on a relatively short passage and reading it in depth. That usually will require several readings. You may even wish to underline some phrases that especially speak to you. You should think of the passage as speaking to you personally. "It requires waiting before the text. You have to take time with it in order to hear what it says." Informational reading involves a problem solving mentality. "In contrast, a characteristic of formational reading is openness to mystery....We come to stand before that Mystery [we call God] and to allow that Mystery to address us. Eventually, we may discover that tremendous problem-solving dynamics emerge out of that encounter. But...we don't enter into the encounter to get problem-solving results." (Mulholland, 53-57).

Formational reading in some respects is far more difficult than informational reading. It requires preparation, a learning how to be still before God, and a willingness to face some of the more painful depths of our lives. Having yielded ourselves to the scripture we "hear" its implications for us in different ways, possibly through imaginative participation in the story, through pondering on the relationship between the event and our own life, through emotional response, painful or joyous, through reinterpretation of a historical perspective into current relevancy, and so on. But it all involves prayer. We are thinking in the presence of God. The initial prayer thoughts may involve more listening than speaking, but spoken prayer as dialogue with God becomes an important part. In the higher moments of this prayer experience we enter into contemplative prayer, resting in the presence of God.

The Community of Christ has available for formative spiritual reading a richness of scriptural material through the Bible, the Book of Mormon, and the Doctrine and Covenants. It encourages response to God's revelatory Spirit through which insights of transforming power become available to those who earnestly seek for understanding. It takes seriously the commission to share with the world "the great and marvelous work" of which each is called to witness.

We invite you during this Lenten season to spend time alone with God in prayer and meditation. The readings assembled here begin with Ash Wednesday and continue through Easter Sunday. Lent traditionally begins on Ash Wednesday, forty days before Easter, excluding Sundays, and ends on Easter Sunday. The organizational structure of the material is derived from the life of Jesus as it impacts our daily lives. It affords each one of us an opportunity to allow the Spirit of Christ to dwell in us. The aim is that we, too, like Paul, will be able to exclaim, "Not I, but Christ in me."

May the Spirit of Christ be your companion on this journey.

A LENTEN TITHE

In many cultures there is an ancient custom of giving a tenth of each year's income to some holy use. For Christians to observe the forty days of Lent is to do the same thing with roughly a tenth of each year's days. After being baptized by John in the river Jordan, Jesus went off alone into the wilderness where he spent forty days asking himself the question what it meant to be Jesus. During Lent, Christians are supposed to ask one way or another what it means to be themselves.

To hear yourself try to answer [this] question...is to begin to hear something not only of who you are but of both what you are becoming and what you are failing to become. It can be a pretty depressing business all in all, but if sackcloth and ashes are at the start of it, something like Easter may be at the end.

Frederich Buechner, *Listening to Your Life*
(HarperSanFrancisco, 1992).

THE CALL OF LENT

Lent is a time to take the time
to let the power of our faith story take hold of us,
a time to let the events
get up and walk around in us,
a time to intensify
our living unto Christ,
a time to hover over
the thoughts of our hearts,
a time to place our feet in the streets of Jerusalem
or to walk along the sea and listen to his word,
a time to touch his robe
and feel the healing surge through us,
a time to ponder and a time to wonder...
Lent is a time to allow a fresh new taste of God!

DAILY WORSHIP
LENT: A SEASON OF CHANGE

The forty days of Lent celebrate the dismembering, disequilibrium and dying that are preludes to the creative transformation of Eastertide. It is a season of being changed and emptied so that new life might come to birth in us and resurrection be found in us as well... Lent is about change: of heart, of perspective, of focus, of the death that precedes life.

Wendy M. Wright, *The Rising*
(Upper Room Books, 1994), 17.

ASH WEDNESDAY A TREASURE IN CLAY VESSELS

Many churches – though not all – celebrate Ash Wednesday with a service in which the sign of the cross in ashes is marked on the forehead with the words, "From dust you came and to dust you will return." It is a diagnostic moment that reminds us of our mortality. Like everything in the universe we will lose our present form. What shall we do with the time we have between then and now? That is what Lent is all about.

* * * * *

So our God fashioned an earth creature out of the clay of the earth and blew into its nostrils the breath of life and the earth creature became a living being.

Gen. 2:7 IHS (Inclusive Hebrew Scriptures)

SCRIPTURE: 2 Cor. 4:6-17; 6:1-3 Transformed Through the Spirit
Jeremiah 18:1-8 The Potter and the Clay
1 Kings 19:4-8 "Get Up and Eat"

ASH WEDNESDAY READINGS:

Therefore since it is by God's mercy that we are engaged in this ministry, we do not lose heart…For it is God who said, "Let light shine out of darkness," who has shone in our hearts to give the light of the knowledge of the glory of God in the face of Christ..

But we have this treasure in clay jars, so that it may be made clear that this extraordinary power belongs to God and does not come from us. We are afflicted in every way, but not crushed, perplexed, but not driven to despair, persecuted, but not forsaken, struck down but not destroyed, because we know that the One who raised the Lord Jesus will bring us with you into his presence.

So we do not lose heart. Even though our outer nature is wasting away, our inner nature is being renewed day by day.

And all of us….seeing the glory of the Lord as though reflected in a mirror are being transformed into the same image from one degree of glory into another, for this comes from the Lord, the Spirit.

(2 Cor. 4: 1, 6-8, 14, 16; 3:18)

The Potter's House

The Lord spoke to Jeremiah and said:

"Come, go down to the potter's house, and there I will let you hear my words." So I went down to the potter's house and there he was working on his wheel. The vessel he was making of clay was spoiled in the potter's hand, and he reworked it into another vessel, as seemed good to him.

Then the word of the Lord came to me, "Can I not do with you, O House of Israel, just as the potter has done?" says the Lord. "Just like the clay in the potter's hand, so are you in my hand."

(Jeremiah 18:1-6).

Walking Toward the Divine Mountain

. . . it is not enough just to know the truth, to have clarity of conviction and to know where ideally our lives should be heading, though that can be a valuable start. There is also the question of heart, of energy, of willpower, of sustaining ourselves on the road. The spiritual life is not a quick sprint to a well-marked finish line, but a marathon, an arduous lifelong journey into an ever-widening horizon. To sustain ourselves on that road, even after we have some assurance that we are on the right road, requires that along the way we continually find what metaphorically might be termed "Elijah's jug," namely the sustenance that God promised to provide to those who are walking the long road toward the divine mountain.

Ronald Rolheiser, *The Holy Longing* (Doubleday, 1999), 214.

"Elijah's Jug"

But he himself went a day's journey into the wilderness, and came and sat down under a solitary broom tree. He asked that he might die. "It is enough, now, O Lord, take away my life, for I am no better than my ancestors." Then he himself went a day's journey into the wilderness and came and sat down under a solitary broom tree. He asked that he might die: "It is enough, now, O Lord, take away my life, for I am no better than my ancestors." Then he lay down under the broom tree and fell asleep. Suddenly an angel touched him and said to him, "Get up and eat." He looked and there at his head was a cake baked on hot stones and a jar of water. He ate and drank, and lay down again. The angel of the Lord came a second time, touched him and said, "Get up and eat, otherwise the journey will be too much for you." He got up and ate and drank, then he went in the strength of that food forty days and forty nights to Horeb, the mount of God.

(1 Kings 19: 4-8).

A Foot of Clay

There is not a single shoe in this place that does not contain a foot of clay, a foot that drags, a foot that stumbles, but on just such feet we all seek to follow that road through a world where there are many other roads to follow, and hardly one of them that is not more clearly marked and easier to tramp and toward an end more known, more assured, more realizable. But we have picked this road, or been picked by it.

Frederick Buechner, "The Road Goes On," *A Room Called Remember* (SanFranciscoHarper, 1992), 144.

On the Road

If {we} cannot be faithful in the hours
Between the joy and underneath the pain.
We will miss the grace which comes so soft and slow,
We will miss God who whispers in the night,
The cloud of witnesses who stand beside

Another shore and in a greater light.
The veil is always parted, if we knew
But where to look, and what to see and how.
Jennifer Lynn Woodruff, *Weavings* (Jan/Feb. 2002).

What is your road like? Do you have the courage to be faithful "in the hours between the joy and underneath the pain"? Who are your companions on the journey?

PRAYER: Creative Spirit,
Why should I doubt that you can shape and mold
the lump of clay that I am
into an earthen vessel suitable for carrying your love?
Why should I doubt that you can transform
what is ugly or evil
into that which is beautiful and good?
Shape me, melt me, mold me
through the touch of your artist's vision
and the energy of your Spirit
into the disciple you yearn for me to be.
Cathy Cummings Chisholm, *Landscapes of the Heart*
(Bridge Resources, 1998) 105.

THURSDAY METANOIA — REPENTANCE

SCRIPTURE: **Psalm 51:1-12 Create in Me a Clean Heart**

Create in me a clean heart, O God, and put a new and right spirit within me.

Romans 12:1-2 Be Ye Transformed

Do not be conformed to this world, but be transformed by the renewing of your minds, so that you may discern what is the will of God – what is good and acceptable and perfect

Ezekiel 36:26 A New Heart

A new heart I will give you, and a new spirit I will put within you; and I will remove from your body the heart of stone and give you a heart of flesh.

MEDITATION: Metanoia

The word translated throughout the New Testament as "repentance" is the Greek "metanoia", which means "change of mind." . . . The particle "meta" indicates transference, or transformation, or beyondness. . . "Noia" is from the Greek word "nous" which means "mind." The word "metanoia," therefore, has to do with transformation of the mind. It refers to a "new mind" – a new way of thinking. (26)

* * * *

{Metanoia] refers to the willingness to change, to be submissive to the Father's loving will and to remove whatever is an obstacle to loving relationship with Him. Actually, we do not have any one English word which adequately expresses the New Testament meaning of metanoia. "Repentance," which is commonly used, means "to be sorry again" rather than a change of thought and purpose, a mental revolution which affects the course of one's life. (Foreword).

Mary Ogden Davis, *Metanoia, A Transformational Journey*
(DeVorss and Company, 1984).

Metanoia — Repentance

But how do we change and how do we clothe ourselves with Christ? There is really only one way: consecration. Consecration is a very special word and involves the most significant promise we make. We can be committed to many things but consecrated only to God. It is a vow made to God that we are willing to walk the path of discipleship with all that means. We make such a vow in the waters of baptism, a promise to remember Christ and keep his commandments that we may have his Spirit to be with us. Keeping the commandments involves more than righteousness. Unless the commandments we follow are infused with the Spirit of the living God there will be little nourishment to sustain us on the journey.

Regardless of how slight may be our contact with God, it is a quality of the experience that our understanding of ourselves is clarified; we become aware of our sinning. Sins are not isolated acts or bad habits except as these grow out of what we basically are. Sin is a tendency of our whole self and character. In the light of the ultimate goal for which we were created; it is the failure to become what we were created to be. Repentance is a dynamic change of heart and involves recognition of our failure and firm purpose of amendment. God does not through miraculous intervention complete the task of our transformation. The decisions, choices, and heroic endeavor of change, though initiated and supported through the Spirit, are ours alone.

Repentance is both a negative and positive experience, death and life. Tennyson wrote in *In Memoriam* that "Men rise on stepping stones/ Of their dead selves to higher things." The negative aspect of repentance is the death of those things that hinder what we are attempting to become. It is a climb up the mountain of self-knowledge and a determination to eradicate whatever causes us to miss the mark of our calling. The positive aspect of repentance is "rising from our dead selves to higher things." The world that we have centered almost entirely around ourselves must open to a transcendent reality. We must find a new center of being. Such centering requires the organization of all our powers in sounding the deeps of love and in learning to do justly, love mercy, and walk humbly before God. It lays claim on the entire person, is a slow process, and costs more than many are willing to give. Yet through it we become part of a larger, enveloping Life with the release of energy and the experience of joy and serenity that accompanies such a transformation.

Velma Ruch

What changes do you feel are necessary in your life? Do you have the willingness to change and the heroic resolve that will make a difference in your lifestyle?

PRAYER: Loving God, you who have borne our griefs and been wounded for our transgressions, we come in repentance for the sins that so easily beset us. With your help we wish to rise on stepping stones of our dead selves to higher things. Restore us to the joy of our salvation. Amen.

FRIDAY PRAYER AND FASTING

SCRIPTURE: **Joel 2:12-13 Rend Your Hearts and Not Your Clothing**

Yet even now says your Lord, return to me with all your heart with fasting, with weeping, and with mourning.

Isaiah 58:6-9 The Fast I Choose

Is not this the fast that I choose: to loose the bonds of injustice, to share your bread with the hungry....

Doctrine and Covenants 59:2d-h; 3a-b That Thy Joy May Be Full

And on this day thou shalt do none other thing, only let thy food be prepared with singleness of heart, that thy fasting may be perfect; or in other words, that thy joy may be full.

MEDITATION: Fasting

Entering into any one of the spiritual disciplines is an adventure with God. This is one reason why it is good for us to have experience with various ones of the spiritual disciplines. We may discover that an approach to the Divine that had never been part of our practice may yield spiritual benefits beyond what we have known before. Any of the disciplines approached in a deep spirit of devotion will yield blessing but some may resonate more powerfully within us than others. It is important for us to discover what these are.

Fasting historically has been one of the most prominent of the disciplines. "The central idea in fasting," Richard Foster writes, "is the voluntary denial of an otherwise normal function for the sake of intense spiritual activity." (Study Guide to *Celebration of Discipline*). There is no question that self-denial is an important aspect of fasting, but whatever is done should be done with a spiritual focus that is clear in one's mind. If we are to engage in fasting it is tremendously important that we know why we are doing it.

A careful reading of Isaiah 58 and Section 59 of the Doctrine and Covenants is very helpful in leading us to understand the important principles involved.

Section 59 of The Doctrine and Covenants is the first mention of fasting in the church. The Section is primarily concerned about the elements that go into saintly living. We discover that there is no one right way to fast. It depends on the spirit with which we do it and how it integrates with the other aspects of saintly living:

Total commitment to God
Love toward God and others
Service
Attitudes toward belongings of others
Gratitude
Living sacrifice – broken heart and contrite spirit
Repentance and forgiveness
Ever deepening life of devotion
Humility
Observing Sabbath rest

In Section 59 we have the heart of the gospel in which fasting plays a part.

True Fasting

True fasting is different from missing a meal or not eating because of poverty. Fasting empties out, makes space, asserts the will against the appetite. It allows for self discovery and openness to God.

In the light of God's love and forgiveness, you are encouraged to discover the part of you that you keep hidden to yourself. The more you discover God's light, the more you discover in yourself the need for that light. It's like hearing God say, "I love you so much I want to touch you in all the places where you are lost, hurt, and broken so that you may know those places but may also know that I find you in those places, too, and want to heal you."

Edith Gallaher

A Time of Prayer

Spending this Lenten time, this time in the desert, is a time of prayer. There is fasting and discernment, introspection and realization, searching and knowing. There is dying and a slow coming to new life, shedding the old and unfitting and putting on the fresh and living. There is plunging into the darkness and there finding that which needs to be reconciled, healed, or discarded. There is discovery and disclosure of self and yielding to become what God has meant for us to be. Jesus entered the desert, but not without prayer, and neither should we. Frances de Sales writes about the necessity of finding the devotional habits that fit our needs. I am reminded by that to pray, but not just any prayer. I need to remember Jesus teaching and find the way to incorporate that in a prayer form best suited for my personality, routine, energy and needs.

Edith Gallaher

What are your thoughts regarding fasting? In what ways have you experienced it? What do you see as the relationship between fasting and prayer? Have you found the fasting and prayer that best ministers to the person you are and the persons for whom you pray? What are they? What do you still hunger for?

PRAYER: Sustain in me a willing spirit, O God , and may my sacrifices before you be given with purity of heart and desire to grow into your likeness. May the consecration of my life be a power for good in the lives of others. Amen.

SATURDAY
SELF-EXAMINATION

SCRIPTURE: **Psalm 139:1-18; 23-24 Search Me, O God.**

Search me, O God, and know my heart; test me and know my thoughts. See if there is any wicked way in me, and lead me in the way everlasting.

MEDITATION: A God of Loving Attentiveness

The image that emerges in the opening lines of Psalm 139 depicts a God who searches us. The word *search* comes from the Latin *circare,* "to go around." God encircles us, then goes around our inner most being, searching and knowing us through and through. The image suggests that God is intimately and integrally involved in our lives . . . .

The God who encircles us does not confine us, however. The psalmist experiences a God who remains present in the depths and heights of human experience: "If I make my bed in Sheol, you are there. If I take the wings of the morning...your hand shall lead me" (vv. 9-10). Even in darkness we do not escape this encircling presence (vv. 11-12). The psalm reveals a God who neither prohibits our freedom nor intervenes in our fleeing, but who watches over us in close, loving attentiveness . . . .

After telling us that God is not limited by time: "For it was you who formed my inward parts; you knit me together in my mother's womb' (v. 13), God has been present and attentive to us since before we were born. The feminine image of God tenderly knitting us together complements the portrait of an omniscient God who moves about and looks over us in what may be thought of as a paternal way. The knitter stays put, creating stitch by stitch the work of her hands . . . . Since we go on developing and growing throughout our lives, this stitching must be an ongoing process. God's knitting is patient prayer, an act of love that brings us being and then sustains us as we continue to become.

The psalmist's recognition of the divine presence leads to the invitation, "Search me, O God, and know my heart, . . . lead me in the way everlasting (vv. 23-24). Perhaps this is the response that God desires from each of us to recognize and affirm God's presence and then to grant God full freedom as an expression of our surrender and trust.

The recognition does not change God: it changes us. God has always encircled and searched and knitted and vanquished fears and will not cease doing so. Our invitation signals that we desire to grow in awareness of God's movements and thus participate in the mystery of God's ongoing prayer.

Judy Cannato, Weavings (May/June, 2002) 40.

God's Words to Jeremiah

Now the word of the Lord came to me saying, "Before I formed you in the womb I knew you, and before you were born I consecrated you, I appointed you a prophet to the nations." Then I said, "Ah, Lord God! Truly, I do not know how to speak, for I am only a boy." Then the Lord said to me, "Do not say, 'I am only a boy'; for you shall go to all to whom I send you, and you shall speak whatever I command you. Do not be afraid of them, for I am with you to deliver you, says the Lord." Then the Lord put out his hand and touched my mouth, and the Lord said to me, "Now I have put my words in your mouth; See, today I appoint you over nations and over kingdoms, to pluck up and to pull down, to destroy and to overthrow, to build and to plant."

(Jeremiah 1: 1-10)

If the Spirit of God were to initiate a conversation with you about who you are and what God longs to see fulfilled in you, what would that conversation be like? If such a sacred moment has already happened to you, how have you been following through?

PRAYER: My Lord God, I have no idea where I am going. I do not see the road ahead of me. I cannot know for certain where it will end. Nor do I really know myself, and the fact that I think that I am following your will does not mean that I am actually doing so. But I believe that the desire to please you does in fact please you. And I hope I have that desire in all that I am doing. I hope that I will never do anything apart from that desire. And I know that if I do this you will lead me by the right road though I may know nothing about it. Therefore will I trust you always though I may seem to be lost and in the shadow of death. I will not fear, for you are ever with me, and you will never leave me to meet my perils alone. Amen.

Thomas Merton, *Thoughts in Solitude*

THE FIRST WEEK OF LENT
THEME: WE PREPARE FOR THE JOURNEY

One small word of counsel before we strike out onto this disciplined journey into the holy place: healthy prayer necessitates frequent experiences of the common, earthy, run-of-the-mill variety. Like walks, and talks, and good wholesome laughter. Like work in the yard, and chitchat with the neighbors, and washing windows. Like loving our spouse, and playing with our kids, and working with our colleagues. To be spiritually fit to scale the Himalayas of the Spirit, we need regular exercise in the hills and valleys of ordinary life.

Richard J. Foster, "Preface," *Prayer*
(Harper San Francisco, 1992), xii.

SUNDAY, THE FIRST WEEK OF LENT: THE HOPE OF THE WORLD

SCRIPTURE: **Isaiah 35:1-8 The Promise**

Then the eyes of the blind shall be opened, and the ears of the deaf be unstopped; then the lame shall leap like a deer and the tongue of the speechless sing for joy.

Isaiah 65:23-25 The Vision

Before they call I will answer, while they are yet speaking I will hear... They shall not hurt or destroy on all my holy mountain.

Isaiah 9:6-7 The Coming King

For a child has been born for us, a son given to us;... and he is named Wonderful Counselor, Mighty God, Everlasting Father, Prince of Peace.

MEDITATION: The Vision of Isaiah

We are the recipients of a promise . . . .How breathtakingly that promise is refracted for us in the texts of Isaiah. The prophet's magnificent vision has always been understood in the Christian community to foretell a new age that is to be ushered in by a messianic savior. And the earliest Christians interpreted these texts in retrospect to refer to Jesus of Nazareth, who was for them the promised one.

Generations of Christians have celebrated and allowed their hope to be enlivened by the messianic proclamation. They have prayed and preached and sung it. What would the pre-Christmas season be without singing along with or at least listening to Handel's Messiah with its contrapuntal setting of Isaiah's words? *For unto us a child is bo-o-o o* . . . Here the sopranos take off on a florid display of agility, and the basses, then the tenors and altos echo back. *Wonderful!* The chorus thunders. *Counselor!* They proclaim again. Then emphatically *The Mighty God!* The combined voices descend down the scale, *The Everlasting Father*, and alight with calm repose upon the dominant tone *The Prince of Peace*.

Music like this gives wings to Christian faith that the promise has its beginning in the birth of a child long ago who was the fulfillment of ancient Israel's prophecies. He was the one who was to give flesh to that startling, counter-cultural vision. . . . .What this startling vision points to is a world transformed: a reality in which injustice and poverty are unknown, where the dispossessed and the vulnerable will be welcomed, where death itself and the inevitable sorrow and labor of life will be no more. This is what we long for, this is what we are promised, this is what has begun.

Wendy M. Wright, *The Vigil*
(Upper Room Books, 1992), 23-25.

Has this messianic vision taken hold of you? Do you attempt to incorporate it in your life? Has the one called *Wonderful! Counselor! The Mighty God! The Everlasting Father! The Prince of Peace!* found an abiding place in your heart?

PRAYER: **On Hearing Handel's Messiah**

Lord, we come rejoicing!
Harpsichord and violin,
choir of your people
brought in fullness
in one body, instrument
and voice wed in celebration.

Oboe, trumpet, tympani
recall your passion,
promise and mystery.
Half note, faith note,
sharp and flat,
resound in your holy name.
Alleluia! Alleluia!

We gather to listen –
voice and instrument
brought into fullness,
brought into glory,
praising, professing,
your magnificent story.

Etched in the Braille of our souls
we finger your names,
whispering them to ourselves
with lips of fire:
Wonderful, Counselor, Mighty God,
Everlasting Father, Prince of Peace.

Alleluia! Alleluia!

Called unto fullness and grace,
called to worship and bless,
we praise your holy name –
eternal mystery revealed

to quiet believers
through living Word become song.

Just as your servant Handel
lay upon your altar
his reverent composition,
so accept our humble gift
of rapt attention,
in honor of your everlasting love.
Alleluia! Alleluia!
Amen.

Phyllis Price, *Holy Fire* (Paulist Press, 1998).

MONDAY, THE FIRST WEEK OF LENT
UNTO YOU A CHILD IS BORN

Holy Night

Long lay the world in sin and error pining
'til he appeared and the soul felt its worth.
A thrill of hope, the weary world rejoices
as yonder breaks a new and glorious morn!

SCRIPTURE: **Luke 1:26-28 Gabriel and Mary**

"Here am I, the servant of the Lord; let it be with me according to your word."

Luke 2:1-20 The Birth of Jesus

"Do not be afraid; for see – I am bringing you good news of great joy for all people: to you is born this day in the city of David, a Savior, who is the Messiah, the Lord."

MEDITATION: Within Your Power of Choosing

Probably no one was less experienced than Mary in the ways of the Divine when on that seemingly ordinary day she was surprised by the appearance of the angel Gabriel. In a Christmas oratorio called *For the Time Being*, the poet W. H. Auden creates his own version of the conversation between Gabriel and Mary. Gabriel says to her:

What I am willed to ask, your own
Will has to answer; child, it lies
Within your power of choosing to
Conceive the Child who chooses you.

That is the basic choice that comes to each of us. We are asked whether we choose to conceive the child that chooses us. Such affirmation cannot be forced. As Eve once chose so Mary had to choose. She did, and answered with full conviction.

About this Joan Chittister has written, "The will of God is something that must be chosen and that costs. The will of God is not a trick played on the unsuspecting. The will of God is always an offer of co-creation. Mary was asked, and Mary said yes." (*Sojourners*, July, 1987, 21). Though Mary may not have totally known what she was saying yes to, she accepted in faith and trust as did Abraham when he departed into the wilderness in response to the revelation of the Divine.

Velma Ruch, *Summoned to Pilgrimage*
(Herald Publishing House, 1994), 46-47.

I wonder as I wander out under the sky
How Jesus our Savior did come for to die
For poor, ornery people like you and like I
I wonder as I wander out under the sky.

When Mary birthed Jesus 'twas in a cow's stall
With wise men and farmers and shepherds and all
But high from the heavens a star's light did fall
And the promise of ages it then did recall.

Appalachian Folk Carol, *Hymns of the Saints,* # 251

Every Child Is Blessed

You are a person who is blessed in your very creation, and this blessing never leaves you. Your challenge is to claim that "original blessing" as a child of the One who gave it to you. If you have been wounded by the original sin, you are healed by the original blessing. The original blessing, the unconditional love of God, was present in God's mind and heart long before your conception. It touches you from before your beginning until after your death. It embraces you forever. You are the blessed one. That is your destiny.

Henri Nouwen, *From Fear to Love: Lenten Reflections on the Parable of the Prodigal Son* (This booklet was edited by Mark Neilsen for Creative Communications for the Parish, Fenton, Mo. 63026. The original material was drawn from a series of audio cassettes entitled "The Return of the Prodigal Son," 1998).

Living As God's Child

If you're a child of God, you are unlike any other person. You are a unique son of God, you are a unique daughter of God. By living your life as a child of God you have a unique statement to make and I encourage you to make it. If you let your life go by not having said anything, you let the world define you as an ordinary person. But the world doesn't need ordinary persons. The world needs witnesses, prophets, teachers, lovers. The people in the human family need people who claim God within them, and speak out by their lives of hope and compassion.

If you claim this identity and live it you must be prepared, because the world will hate you and will laugh at you and will make fun of you. But if you know who you are as a son or daughter of God, and if you're linked into a community of believers, you will grow and give hope to brothers and sisters everywhere.

Nouwen, *ibid*, 15.

Have you ever asked yourself who you were created to be and what unique statement is yours to make? How is it going? What have you discovered? Have you sung the song you came to sing or do you empathize with Tagore in the poem below?

The Song I Came to Sing

The song that I came to sing remains unsung to this day. I have spent
my days in stringing and in unstringing my instrument.
The time has not come true. The words have not been rightly set; only
there is the agony of wishing in my heart.
The blossom has not opened; only the wind is sighing by.
I have not seen his face, nor have I listened to his voice;
only I have heard his gentle footsteps from the road before my house.
The livelong day has passed in spreading his seat on the floor; but the
lamp has not been lit and I cannot ask him into my house.
I live in hope of meeting with him but that meeting is not yet.

Rabindranath Tagore, *Gitanjali* , Poem 13
(International Pocket Library)

Meditate on the Following Scriptures:

We all reflect as in a mirror the splendor of the Lord; thus we are transfigured into his likeness, from splendor to splendor (2 Cor. 3: 18 New English Bible).

Surely you know that you are God's temple, where the Spirit of God dwells... The temple of God is holy, and that temple you are (1 Cor. 3:16-17 NEB).

Each man should examine his own conduct for himself; then he can measure his achievement by comparing himself with himself and not with anyone else (Gal. 6: 4-5 NEB).

You are precious in my eyes, and honored and I love you (Isaiah 43:4).

PRAYER:

Make room within my heart, O God, That you may form in me
The image you have shown in Christ, My very life to be.
Inspire my thought, O Lofty One, To reach the highest plane,
That I may know the mind of Christ, And him as greatest gain.

Bryan Jeffery Leech, *Hymns of the Saints,* # 182.

TUESDAY, THE FIRST WEEK OF LENT
GROWING IN WISDOM AND STATURE

SCRIPTURE: **Luke 2:41-52 The Boy Jesus at the Temple**

"Why were you searching for me? Did you not know that I must be in my Father's house?"

Matthew 18:1-5 Unless You Become Like a Little Child

"Truly I tell you, unless you change and become like children you will never enter the kingdom of heaven."

MEDITATION: The Hidden Years

We are given very little information about [Jesus'] growing up years, but what we are given is highly suggestive. . . . Following the birth events we are told quite straightforwardly that "the child grew and became strong, filled with wisdom; and the favor of God was upon him" (Luke 2:40). A parallel statement is given later, following Jesus' interaction with the leading teachers in the temple when he was twelve: "And Jesus increased in wisdom and in years, and in divine and human favor" (Luke 2:52). Most instructive of all is the simple comment of Luke after Joseph and Mary had found Jesus in the temple "Then [Jesus] went down with them and came to Nazareth, and was obedient to them" (Luke 2:51).

A whole world is carried in that unadorned observation that Jesus was "obedient to them." Jesus grew up under the tutelage of his parents, Joseph and Mary. And while Joseph is not heard from again, we can be confident that Jesus learned the carpentry trade from him and worked in that trade until he began his public ministry at roughly the age of thirty.

We would do well to ponder those years Jesus spent as a carpenter, working in what we today would call a blue-collar job. Where do you imagine Jesus learned to walk in perfect harmony with his heavenly Father? Where do you imagine he came to experience such a life of single-minded devotion to God that he knew that "no one can serve two masters" (Matt. 6:24)? Where, I ask you, did he learn such a deep, intimate life of prayer that he could confidently teach us, "Ask and it will be given you; search, and you will find, knock, and the door will be opened for you. For everyone who knocks, the door will be opened" (Matt7:7)? Where do you think he learned to live out the words, "In everything do to others as you would have them do to you" (Matt. 7:12)? Where did he learn all these things and so much more? I will tell you where. He learned them in his carpentry work and at home with his parents and his brothers and sisters. Jesus did not all of a sudden one day start spouting nice sayings about God. No, when he began his public ministry, he was speaking out of a life that had been tested and tried. He had proven the teachings to be true over and over again as he sawed wood and assembled chairs and built cabinets.

Richard J. Foster, *Streams of Living Water, 19-20.*

Principles of Growth

Growth means development in the life of an organism. It means change manifest in structure. In highly developed organisms such as man, growth means change in structure and quality of character. . . . For our purposes here growth means the orderly process of development through which a form of life goes from seed to fruit, from egg to matured animal, from cell to embryo to adult human being. It will be our task to explore some of the ways in which the growth of human beings yields or makes for the kind of discipline in the individual that is essentially spiritual in character.. . . Growth provides raw material which can be used in that way. What is taking place at the level of the physical organism may find its counterpart in the life of the mind and the spirit (38-39).

* * * * *

[In growth a person] is driven back upon one of the most ancient insights of religion: that there is a Purpose that invades all his purposes and a Wisdom that invades all his wisdoms. To seek to relate oneself to such a purpose and such a wisdom is to seek to know God and to walk in His Way. The discipline of growth becomes the discipline of the spirit, and the increase in stature and wisdom can mean a growth in the knowledge of God and the understanding of His Kingdom. Thus the Master teaches us that if we seek the Kingdom and His righteousness, all else will be ours. We will not be guaranteed against failure, but we will learn that we may fail again and again and yet be assured always that we are not mistaken in what we affirm with all our hearts and minds. The prayer of the Psalmist becomes our prayer: "Thou compassest my path and my lying down, and art acquainted with all my ways. ...Search me, O God . . . try me, and know my thoughts and see if there be any wicked way in me, and lead me in the Way everlasting." (63).

Excerpts from Howard Thurman, "Growing in Wisdom and Stature," *Disciplines of the Spirit* (Friends United press, 1977).

The Signet of Eternity

The day was when I did not keep myself in readiness for thee; and
entering my heart unbidden even as one of the common crowd,
unknown to me, my king, thou didst press the signet of eternity
upon many a fleeting moment of my life.
And today when by chance I light upon them and see thy
Signature, I find they have lain scattered in the dust mixed with
the memory of joys and sorrows of my trivial days forgotten.
Thou didst not turn in contempt from my childish play among
dust, and the steps that I heard in my playroom are the same
that are echoed from star to star.

Rabindranath Tagore, *Gitanjali,* Poem 43,
(International Pocket Library)

Unless You Become As A Little Child

The truths we recognize as children are of a special quality. We are filled with wonder, and it is not difficult on the wings of a child's dreaming to feel a part of all that is. We identify with and become part of the mystery of being. There is a great deal of gladness at the heart of that mystery, a gladness we accept but whose source we do not fully comprehend. We experience in these special awakening moments of childhood a joy not too dissimilar from that of Milton's Adam after his creation. Adam tells of coming to consciousness lying "soft on the flow'ry herb." His "wondering eyes" turned toward heaven, and by "quick, instinctive motion" up he sprung and stood upright. He looked around and saw "hill, dale, and shady woods and sunny plain." There were "Creatures that liv'd and mov'd, and walk'd, or flew" and "Birds on the branches warbling." He continues his account to the Angel Raphael:

All things smil'd
With fragrance and with joy my heart o'erflow'd.
But who I was, or where, or from what cause,
Knew not; to speak I tri'd and forthwith spake,
My tongue obey'd and readily could name
Whate'er I saw. Thou Sun, said I, fair Light,
And thou enlight'n'd Earth, so fresh and gay,
Ye Hills and Dales, ye Rivers, Woods, and Plains
And ye that live and move; fair Creatures, tell,
Tell, if ye saw, how came I thus, how here?
Not of myself; by some great Maker then,
In goodness and in power preeminent;
Tell me, how may I know him, how adore,
From whom I have that thus I move and live,
And feel that I am happier than I know.

Paradise Lost, Book 8

It seems to me that the joy experienced by the newly created, wondering Adam is very like that we know as children. The innocence of childhood becomes a clear and open channel for joy. C. S. Lewis wrote of similar experiences in his autobiography, *Surprised by Joy.* From the time he was very young, Lewis had mystical experiences of the presence of God. To these he later applied the word "joy." As his biographer writes, "He valued these experiences of joy more than anything else he had known, and he desired, as all who have experienced them desire, to have them again and again. . . . He was surprised by joy. He spent the rest of his life searching for more of it." (George Sayer, *Jack: C. S. Lewis and His Times,* 21).

Distinguished Author Lectures, 1988-1989.
Velma Ruch, "My Heart Was Full."
(Herald Publishing House, 1989), 50-51.

What are your memories of childhood? Do you still maintain the wonder and openness of a child? What qualities do you think Jesus had in mind when he said, "Truly I tell you, unless you change and become like children, you will never enter the kingdom of heaven"?

PRAYER: Gracious Spirit, dwell with me,
I myself would holy be;
And with words that help and heal
Would thy life in mine reveal;
And with actions bold but meek
Would for Christ my Savior speak.
Truthful Spirit, dwell with me.
I myself would truthful be;
And with wisdom kind and clear
Let thy life in mine appear;
And with actions neighborly
Speak my Lord's sincerity.

Thomas T. Lynch. *Hymns of the Saints,* # 284.

WEDNESDAY, THE FIRST WEEK OF LENT: PREPARING THE WAY

SCRIPTURE: **Luke 1:76-80 Zechariah's Prophecy**

"And you, child, will be called the prophet of the Most High; for you will go before the Lord to prepare his ways, to give knowledge of salvation to his people."

Luke 3:1-6 John the Baptist Prepares the Way

"The voice of one crying out in the wilderness: 'Prepare the way of the Lord, make his paths straight...and all flesh shall see the salvation of God.'"

MEDITATION: John the Baptist

John the forerunner, the one who prepares the way, retains a respected place in our cumulative imagination. We envision him as a tiny infant, the much-wanted son of an elderly barren couple, whose birth was from the beginning surrounded by the aura of prophecy and miracle, proclaimed prophet of the Most High by his own father, the one who will prepare the way for the promised coming of a new dawn. We have wanted to see him, as in our paintings of the "holy kinship," as a ruddy toddler playing with his infant cousin Jesus, secure in the domestic comfort of Elizabeth and Mary's care. We have pictured John as a young ascetic, gripped in the zealousness of his prophetic vocation, the locust-eating, camel's-hair-clad wild man crying aloud in the wilderness, "Prepare a way for the Lord!" Surrounded by his crowd of followers, we have imagined him knee deep in the Jordan , urging all to repent and be baptized. We depict him pouring waters over Jesus' head, demurring, exclaiming that their roles should be reversed, knowing himself as not worthy even to tie the strap of Jesus' sandal. Finally we call up our final image of this man, John, his severed head upon a platter served up to the delight of Herod's family, a victim of his own moral denunciation.. . .

"Prepare ye," he heralds. "Make straight the path." Such preparation as a spiritual discipline, has almost nothing in common with the busy, frenetic preparations with which we fill our days before the Christmas season. Such preparation has to do with emptying, not filling, with making space rather than crowding it, with letting go, not stocking up. Little must be enough. Otherwise, where in our lives is there room for God?

Wendy M. Wright, *The Time Between*
(Upper Room Books, 1999), 113-115.

Obstinate Are the Trammels

Obstinate are the trammels, but my heart aches when I try to break them.
Freedom is all I want, but to hope for it I feel ashamed.
I am certain that priceless wealth is in thee, and that thou art my best friend,
    but I have not the heart to sweep away the tinsel that fills my room.
The shroud that covers me is a shroud of dust and death;
I hate it, yet hug it in love.
My debts are large, my failures great, my shame secret and heavy;
Yet when I come to ask for my good, I quake in fear
    lest my prayer be granted.

Rabindranath Tagore, *Gitanjali,* Poem 28.

How are you preparing for the coming of the Lord into your life? Who were the messengers that led the way for you?

PRAYER:

I long for your presence, O God.
In the midst of my estrangement I seek to be connected.
Connected to you, connected to others, connected to self.
Why is it that I am so far from you?
What has caused this isolation of my heart?
How did my journey take me to this barren wasteland of loneliness?
I believe in your grace,
I believe in your need for my presence with you.
I believe in our partnership in all creative acts.
Give me courage, dear Friend, and insight too.
Courage and insight sufficient to explore the voids.
Courage and insight to understand my need for transformation,
Courage and insight to once again become intimate –
Intimate with you and all your beautiful creation.

Kenneth McLaughlin

THURSDAY, THE FIRST WEEK OF LENT: IMMERSED IN THE WATER

SCRIPTURE: **Matthew 3:13-17; Luke 3:21-22 The Baptism of Jesus**

And when Jesus had been baptized, just as he came up from the water, suddenly the heavens were opened to him and he saw the Spirit of God descending like a dove and alighting on him, And a voice from heaven said, "This is my Son, the Beloved, with whom I am well pleased."

Book of Mormon, Mosiah 9:39-42; 48-49 The Waters of Mormon

And they were baptized in the waters of Mormon and were filled with the grace of God

MEDITATION: **Jesus Prays**

My father who are in heaven
as I walk the path
of my purpose on earth
my thoughts return to the night
in the stable
when first I looked into Mary's eyes
and felt the rough hand
of Joseph the carpenter
tenderly cradle my head.
The strong smell of earth and animals
filled my newborn nostrils,
but even then it was water
that called to me.

Going down to the Jordan I am greeted
by the scent of wet camel's hair.
It stings like that of the animals
at my birth
and envelopes John like an aura.
Stretching out his hand
he draws me into the river
fulfilling the words of the Prophet.
And you, my Abba, my Father,
Proclaim your love and blessing.
On the bank of the river the Baptist John
kneels to tie my sandal straps.

Phyllis Price, *Mary's Child.* (manuscript in process).

Baptism Day

All eyes of the crowd are riveted on [John]. People wonder if this could be the one sent from God to save them, their land, their nation. But John announces "I baptize you with water. Among you stands one whom you do not know, the one who is coming after me; I am not worthy to untie the thong of his sandal" (Luke 3:16)....Quietly, almost unnoticed, a man begins to move from the back of the crowd. He walks down the bank and wades into the river to be baptized. John assists him into the waters of the Jordan. As the man emerges from the water, he raises his hands in prayer, and he looks up to the sky. The skies have been drawn back, as though an unseen hand has pulled aside the shimmering curtain of blue, revealing heaven! Shining, light, beautiful, inviting. The waters of the river have not parted, but heaven has been opened. A dove descends from this shining beauty, wings its way downward to the place where all stand transfixed, and gently settles on the shoulder of this man who stands in front of John. Another voice sounds, but not from the wilderness. This voice speaks from heaven: 'You are my Son, the Beloved; with you I am well pleased.'" (Mark 1-11). 61-62.

Wendy J. Miller, *Jesus, Our Spiritual Director*
(Upper Room Books, 2004)

Benediction

A child was born.
A mother was exhausted.
A father stood watch.
Angels sang.
Shepherds left their flocks.
A star appeared
Wise ones from the East paid homage.
An Evangelist cried in the wilderness.
A way was prepared.
Jesus from Nazareth stepped into the River Jordan.
A voice from heaven declared: "This is my beloved."
And nothing was ever the same again.
Not for them. Not for us. Not even for God.

So then, may Jesus, our Brother, who by his incarnation
Gathered into one, things earthly and heavenly,
Fill you with the sweetness of inward peace and outward
goodwill.

May the blessing of God,
The love of Christ,
And the Fellowship of the Holy Spirit be with you now
And remain with you always.
And the congregation said: **AMEN.**

Helen Bruch Pearson Smith, Third Annual
Seminary Convocation, January 9, 2005

Being Born of Water and Spirit

Though in baptism we arise out of the water in newness of life, that newness is a process that continues for the duration of our earthly existence. Quietly and without fanfare, the Spirit works its miracles in us. The seed is planted, our stubborn natures submit, and slowly, perhaps almost imperceptibly, the fruits of the Spirit grow in us – "love, joy, peace, patience, kindness, generosity, faithfulness, gentleness, and self control." And we learn to do justly, to love mercy, and to walk humbly with our God. We become sacrament. . . . .

For all of us the remembrance of our baptism is in some respects a bittersweet experience. We remember the early glow, the hopes, and the dreams, but we also remember how often we have failed to live the life to which we committed ourselves. What we need to realize is that our dying to sin and rising to grace continues all of our lives. We are engaged in a process of Exodus, moving forward from the old, but often casting longing glances back to what we had, back to the fleshpots of Egypt. We find ourselves tempted and bow down before the golden calf that entices us. We sometimes find that what was once a burning fire in us has grown cold and dull. We begin to wonder if that to which we have committed ourselves is, after all, a chimera, a vain or idle fancy that will disappear and leave us nothing. It is at those times that the redeeming love of Christ comes to us as it once did to Peter when he came walking to Christ on the water, suddenly lost faith and began sinking beneath the waves but there was Jesus unwilling that this dear man he loved should be lost beneath the waves reached out his hand and helped him back into the boat.

Where would any of us be if we, too, at such moments had not experienced the outstretched hand of the Master, "Here, child, get in the boat." Here, son, daughter, there are more sheep to feed."

Taken from Velma Ruch,
Summoned to Pilgrimage, 138-140.

Learning to Live by Love

The vows that we make when we become members of the Church of Jesus Christ are more than an oath to stick around with a particular group of people. I believe that they can be interpreted as a commitment to a total inner transformation. 'The only thing that counts is new creation!' (Gal. 6:15 NEB) This transformation which takes place as we try to live out our lives with those who are also called to be on this inward path, is simply learning to live by love – learning to be persons in community with other persons. This is the most creative and difficult work to which any of us will ever be called. There is no higher achievement in all the world than to be a person in community, and this is the call of every Christian. We are to be builders of liberating communities that free love in us and free love in others.

Elizabeth O'Connor, *Weavings*
(September/October, 1996).

Can you remember your own baptism? What were your feelings then? Recall various seasons in your journey of discipleship. Have you ever been touched by the love of Christ and heard the invitation, "Here, son, daughter, get in the boat"?

PRAYER: In the joy of baptism, O God, we felt the graciousness of your love and consecrated ourselves to a life of discipleship. May we never forget as we follow your footsteps along the way. Amen.

FRIDAY, THE FIRST WEEK OF LENT: LED INTO THE WILDERNESS

SCRIPTURE: **Matthew 4:1-11 Jesus in the Wilderness**

Then Jesus was led up by the Spirit into the wilderness to be tempted by the devil.

Deuteronomy 8:1-10 In the Wilderness with God

Remember the long way that the Lord your God has led you these forty years in the wilderness, in order to humble you, testing you to know what was in your heart.

MEDITATION: The Temptation of Jesus

The wilderness of Judea
lay before him in the noonday sun,
golden as his mother's fresh-baked bread.
The leather of his sandals
brushed against stones on the hillsides
as he walked. Everywhere the desert
was dry, but filled with life.
"My Father, why must I thirst and hunger
these 40 days, for they are as the 40 years
of Moses and the Israelites in the desert.
When shall Satan ever leave me!
He follows me like a wild animal,
longing to devour anyone who has
the scent of righteousness about him.
Never shall I turn these stones into bread!
Never shall I stumble and fall
nor test you to please him!
Never shall this Satan be my god!"

At last the devil departed from him.
Weary and weakened Jesus lay down.
Angels knelt at his head and feet to comfort him.
He slept and dreamed of the Jordan
and heard again his Father's voice: *Beloved.*
At dawn, filled with the Spirit, *ruah*
He rose and left the desert.

Phyllis Price, *Mary's Child* (manuscript in process).

Transfiguration and Temptation

It is perhaps after our spiritual awakening, after we have been commissioned by the Lord and joyfully set out on our journey, that our temptation to betrayal becomes very strong. Christ experienced a supreme moment at the time of his baptism As Mark writes, "Just as he was coming up out of the water, he saw the heavens torn apart and the Spirit descending like a dove on him. And a voice came from heaven, 'You are my Son, the Beloved ; with you

I am well pleased'" (Mark 1:10-11). What a gratifying moment of recognition and choosing! But amazingly, when Jesus returned from the Jordan, "full of the Holy Spirit," he was immediately led by that same Spirit into the wilderness to be tempted. Satan played a major role in this temptation, but the whole process was under the impulse of the Holy Spirit.

Christ in his human form was taught a lesson that would be well for us to heed. It is precisely through our high moments, in the times that we feel most closely linked to the Divine, that our most revealing temptations occur. We feel a new power and a new energy. How easy it is to use them for personal aggrandizement, to believe the power is of our own making rather than a gift bestowed upon us by God. How difficult in this moment of supreme pride—and the pride is legitimate since no greater honor can be bestowed then to have communion with the Divine—to have radical humility at the same time; to recognize that we have no life save it be through dedicated service to God.

The temptations and trials in the wilderness teach us to let go of the separate ego and understand ourselves as servants of broader purposes. It is a stripping process, not only of the facades we have built as a protection of the self, but a stripping of all dependence on outer forms and structures. We are in the desert and we partake of its hunger and thirst. But it is also there that renewal and revelation occur and we are fit to continue our pilgrimage as disciples of the Divine.

Velma Ruch, *Summoned to Pilgrimage,* 18-19.

A Time of Suitability Testing

After the high moment of calling, it is not unusual to spend some time in the wilderness as Christ did following his baptism. James Forbes has written in *Preaching and the Holy Spirit* that it is "a time of suitability testing in which we face the pressures we will encounter in the work that lies ahead. It is the time in our development to seek clarity about our mission." (36). It is usually a time of pain and struggle, one that not all survive. The pain and even sense of unworthiness can lead to refusal of the supreme task of our lives. We wonder, Why should I make the effort? Why should I sacrifice? Why should I expose myself in this way? But if we win through, we know a great deal more about spiritual maturity.

It is important to note that Christ's sojourn in the wilderness was followed by the ministry of angels. To quote Forbes once more, "The ministry of angels is heavenly refreshment after such an ordeal. It is the balm of Gilead that soothes the weary traveler along the way. It is release from pain and relaxation of tense muscles. It is an uplift of spirit . . . It is time for recharging for the liberating activity that is about to begin."

Velma Ruch

Have you in your own experience found yourself in the wilderness after a high moment of calling? Think back on that experience. Were you troubled by the dark? How was survival possible for you? Have there been other experiences of suffering and darkness for you when you may have cried out, "Where are you God?" Did you receive an answer then or perhaps later? Have you experienced "the ministry of angels"?

PRAYER: Loving Lord, search our hearts. Turn our weakness to strength. Grant us the gift of wilderness time where we can be rid of all temptation. Remind us of your gift of living water that we may ever turn to you for drink. Amen.

SATURDAY, THE FIRST WEEK OF LENT: "REMEMBER ME AND KEEP MY COMMANDMENTS"

SCRIPTURE: **Doctrine and Covenants 17:22 d; 23 b Communion Prayers**

. . . and witness unto thee, O God, the Eternal Father, that they are willing to take upon them the name of the Son, and always remember him and keep his commandments which he has given them, that they may always have his Spirit to be with them. Amen.

Matthew 22:36-40 The Great Commandment

"You shall love the Lord your God with all your heart and with all your soul, and with all your mind. This is the greatest and first commandment. And a second is like it: 'You shall love your neighbor as yourself.' On these two commandments hang all the law and the prophets."

MEDITATION: The Remembrance of God

"Everywhere and always God is with us, near to us and in us," writes Theophan the Recluse, the great nineteenth century Russian spiritual master. "But we are not always with Him, since we do not remember Him..."The call and commitment to remember constitute the great antiphon of covenant intimacy between God and the people of God. At the time of the great flood, God declares: "I will remember my covenant that is between me and you and every living creature of all flesh (Gen. 9:15 NRSV). The words of the psalmist express generations of determined faith: "I will call to mind the deeds of the Lord. I will remember you deeds of old" (Ps. 7:11). Paul's crisp summary of the good news invites Timothy into the ancient practice of remembrance: "Remember Jesus Christ, raised from the dead, a descendent of David — that is my gospel" (2 Tim. 2:8) Abba Orsisios, one of the early desert Fathers, employs the image of an oil lamp to convey the dangers of spiritual forgetfulness:

"It is like a lamp filled with oil and lit; if you forget to replenish the oil, gradually it goes out and eventually darkness will prevail."

The remembrance of God brings God to mind but also stirs in us the desire to be with God. Usually this desire expresses itself in a life of deepening prayer. Prayer and the remembrance of God are intertwined. ....The farther we penetrate into the province of prayer, the more we thirst for prayer's deepest purpose and fulfillment: ever fuller communion with God.

John Mogabgab, "Editor's Introduction,"
Weavings (May/June, 1995).

Obedience and Love

Obedience and love can never be separated. Whenever we talk about keeping the commandments, we are talking about love. Any time we obey someone out of fear or duty or some other reason, unless that obedience is accompanied by love, it is hollow. When we speak of obeying the commandments of God, we are speaking of doing so because we love. Also that love is a two-way street: we love God because God first loved us.

How many times in our own lives have we practiced obedience without love? Have you ever bargained with God? "God, if you will do this one thing for me I will go to church every Sunday" or some such statement. How many times have you obeyed, fearing the consequences if you did not. Somehow, you think, 'I have to earn God's love by being good or if I don't behave myself I might go to hell. God has made promises to me, and he is bound if I obey the commandments. So, I will be good for the sake of the reward." And we could go on. "To always remember him and keep his commandments" is no simple statement.

Velma Ruch

Prayer:

Have mercy
Upon us.
Have mercy
Upon our efforts
That we
Before Thee,
In love and in faith,
Righteousness and humility,
May follow Thee,
With self-denial, steadfastness and courage,
And meet Thee
In the silence.

Give us a pure heart
That we may see Thee,
A humble heart
That we may hear Thee,
A heart of love
That we may serve Thee,
A heart of faith
That we may live Thee.
Thou
Whom I do not know
But Whose I am.
Thou
Whom I do not comprehend
But Who has dedicated me
To my destiny.
Thou -- .

Dag Hammerskjold, *Markings,* 214-215

THE SECOND WEEK OF LENT
THEME: BEING SHAPED AND TRANSFORMED

THE SECOND SUNDAY OF LENT: EARLY ENCOUNTERS

SCRIPTURE: **John 1:35-42 Come and See**

The next day John again was standing with two of his disciples and as he watched Jesus walk by, he exclaimed, "Look, here is the Lamb of God!" The two disciples heard him say this and they followed Jesus. When Jesus turned and saw them following he said to them, "What are you looking for?" They said to him, "Rabbi, where are you staying?" He said to them, "Come and see."

Doctrine and Covenants 159:8 Seeing Anew

Then, as you gain ever more confidence in sensing the leadings of my Spirit, you will begin to see with new eyes, embrace the truths that are waiting for your understanding, and move joyfully toward the fulfillment of the tasks that are yours to accomplish.

MEDITATION: "Come and See"

"What do you want?" (John 1:38, JB). Here is the question that searches the depths of human existence, asked by the one who knows those depths as no other. The disciples of John the Baptist to whom Jesus addressed these words must have felt their enormous spiritual resonance. These were followers of the desert prophet, seekers who surely knew the sweet anguish of holy desire inflaming muscle and bone, imagination and will....And you, surely you are not a stranger to the bold quest of desire for what alone will satisfy its ardent longing. What do you want?

A vast arc of desire stretches across human existence, a long sweep of mutual longing between Creator and creature that constitutes the innermost dynamism of history….."Where do you live?" ask John's disciples when they encounter the Son of God. Expressed in the disciples' words are the many urgent, bewildered, painful questions concerning the whereabouts of God in a harsh world. And to these words, in their simplicity and gravity, Jesus responds with the great invitation to all spiritual seekers: "Come and see."

"Come," Jesus says, calling us to step away from personal attitudes, cultural values, even religious convictions that hinder recognition of the God who is closer than we think. How God must cherish our company to number the hairs on our head and to decipher the inarticulate groaning of our soul (Rom 8:22-27). And if indeed God is sometimes hidden, it is not to deny our desire for God's presence but to hallow and intensify it. Freshly roused thirst for God may be precisely the way we discover the invitation to come and see.

John S. Mogabgab, "Editor's Introduction,"
Weavings (January/February, 2004), 2.

Have you ever agonized over where God is in this bewildering, painful, and harsh world? Has the gentle call "Come" ever penetrated your inner being and given you hope?

Early Encounters – A Testimony

As a child of six in Kirtland Temple I experienced my first conscious recognition of being enfolded in the Divine embrace. As someone sang the hymn "In the Garden" and I heard the words of the chorus, "And he walks with me/ And he talks with me/ And he tells me I am his own," I knew it was so. In the warmth of love that flooded my child's heart I knew what I would later call the Spirit as Fire.

At the age of seven in the Stone Church, I experienced the Spirit as Revelatory Voice. My parents and I were preparing to return to Scandinavia and we were invited to participate in a service in which we were each blessed. My blessing was given by Brother Elbert A. Smith. The voice of assurance came that though I would have to change languages and cultures and schools, I would be blessed to overcome the difficulties. In miraculous ways I found it to be so, not only as a child, but as a minister to Norway in my retirement years.

At the age of eight, I was ready for baptism and experienced the Spirit as Cleansing Water. After my baptism in the sunshine of a Norwegian July day, I remember running up a hill from the river feeling so light and clean, and wanting to stay that way.

In the years that have followed I have experienced the Spirit as Dove, as the renewing peace that has come even in the midst of my failures and unworthiness. I was invited in when my actions could well have shut me out.

The Spirit has come to me as Light, illuminating my studies and shining on me from the pages of reading and the radiant faces of the Saints of God.

Through my ordination to priesthood I have been blessed by the Spirit in Anointing Power and have discovered in how many ways God goes before us, preparing hearts for ministry, opening doors, and empowering those he calls to special service.

In the years of diminishment now before me as age and declining health begin to take their toll, I feel more surely than I have ever felt before a richness of Divine presence. I trust that, as Paul expressed it, "the one who began a good work among you will carry it to completion" (Philippians 1:6). Diminishment is not diminishment when it is so. It is rather to know the fullness of being of which Paul also spoke.

Velma Ruch, "Sensing the Leading of My Spirit," *Herald* (September, 1995), 5.

What is your testimony? Take some time to review your own encounters with the Spirit.

PRAYER: Loving Jesus, we cannot forget our early encounters with your Spirit. Along the way you have indeed walked with us and talked with us. May we ever be alert to your voice as it speaks to us and be aware of your presence as it abides in us. Amen.

MONDAY, THE SECOND WEEK OF LENT: "COME AND FOLLOW"

SCRIPTURE: **Mark 1:16-20 The Calling of the First Disciples**

As Jesus passed along the Sea of Galilee, he saw Simon and his brother Andrew casting a net into the sea – for they were fishermen. And Jesus said to them, "Follow me and I will make you fish for people." And immediately they left their nets and followed him.

Doctrine and Covenants 119:8 b All Are Called

All are called according to the gifts of God unto them.

Doctrine and Covenants 4 If You Have Desires You Are Called

...therefore, if ye have desires to serve God, ye are called to the work.

MEDITATION: Fisher of Folk

Fisher of Folk,
Sometimes I'd rather be the one left behind at the dock.
But how can I refuse your call?
You summon me to step out of my past
  to follow you into an unknown future.
You ask me to walk away from contentment
  with my life as it is.
You ask me to sever ties that confine me
  to things that falsely promise security.
You compel me to lift up my eyes to see beyond my fears.
You invite me to follow your example:
  to trust wholeheartedly
  to give sacrificially
  to love unconditionally
  to serve selflessly.
You know the only way I can do all this is to know that I can't
  not on my own, not without you.
Grant me the courage to answer your call wherever it may lead.

Cathy Cummings Chisholm, *Landscapes of the Heart*
(Louisville: Bridge Resources, 1998,) 11.

Christian Leadership

A Christian leader is a person who feels called by God through Christ to expend his or her center life and strength channeling and manifesting this transforming love of God on the frontier where creation meets chaos.

You are a Christian leader if you feel thus called, whether you are in charge of the choir or in charge of the Conference. If you teach a class , work on the finance board, call on the sick, join an intercessory prayer group, work on problems of hunger and injustice, delegate at a conference, concern yourself with the poor, or prepare a worship service, you are a Christian leader.

The ordained minister expresses this calling through full-time professional work. But the lay person responding to the inner call through varying gifts is no less a Christian leader, sharing many of the same rewards and stresses.

Flora Slosson Wuellner, *Prayer, Stress, and Our Inner Wounds.* In *Alive Now* (March/April 1998) 8.

The Call Is for Everyone

In our understanding of the member/minister work of the church, Section 4 of the Doctrine and Covenants is basic. After announcing the marvelous work about to come forth among us, it goes on to speak of the meaning of service and discipleship. We are called to serve with all our heart, might, mind, and strength. We do not have to wait for a call to office: ". . . if ye have desires to serve God, ye are called to the work" (1c) Desire initiates the call, but what qualifies us to serve is first of all the fruits of the Spirit: faith, hope, charity, love, an eye single to the glory of God, virtue, knowledge, temperance, patience, brotherly kindness, godliness, humility diligence. Beyond that is development of competence. No one is exempt from the call or from developing competence in their areas of ministry.

The Uninterrupted Call

God's call is mysterious; it comes in the darkness of faith. It is so fine, so subtle, that it is only with the deepest silence within us that we can hear it. And yet nothing is so decisive and overpowering for a man or woman on this earth, nothing surer or stronger. This call is uninterrupted: God is always calling us! But there are distinctive moments in this call of his, moments which leave a permanent mark on us – moments which we never forget.

Carlo Carretto, *Letters from the Desert* (Orbis, 1972) xv.

Hearing God

God's call cannot be manipulated or shaped by human hands but must be obeyed without any certain knowledge about where it will lead. Therefore, its way is always dark, lighted only by a tiny flicker of faith that creates enough courage for one step at a time.

Why do we think that God always shouts? Could it be that our insensitivity so dulls our hearing that God must shout to get our attention. Once God has gotten our attention, then comes the silence, the inner stillness of the soul that attends the Voice. In its essence the Voice speaks with gentleness and softness so that we must listen intently to hear its message.

How does this subtle, gentle voice speak with such power? How does it enter our lives with such undeniable strength and turn us in new directions that precipitate choices that change us forever? Nothing else changes us so completely as the call of God. It re-orients our whole life. The call leaves within us the residue of certitude that gives us the strength to face the doubts and struggles that are bound to come our way.

Are you feeling a call? Do you wish to answer it and get the decision over with? I have news for you. This simply won't happen. You will never finish with this call! The call of God comes long before you hear it, it lingers until you name it, and then it never completely goes away. Call is continuous! God is always calling us. One distinctive, unforgettable moment comes when you answer the call. But there will be other moments that will come again and again, marking your way and giving you the assurance that the God who called still calls.

Being chosen by God and given a place in the divine mission to the world carries with it a distinction that only the called – both clergy and lay –can fully appreciate!

Ben Campbell Johnson, *Hearing God's Call*
(William B. Eerdmans Publishing Company, 2002) 11-12.

All Are Called

In our church we have had some difficulty in relating a hierarchical approach to priesthood with the "all are called" doctrine. Priesthood is a focused ministry in which through the call of God, approval of the people, and ordination, individuals are called to fairly specific ministries in terms of their giftedness. But one thing the apostle Paul made abundantly clear – a position reaffirmed in Restoration scripture (Section 46) – is that every disciple of Christ has at least one spiritual gift. We are a body, with each member important to the well-being of the whole. Even the most mature of us has need of "The least of these." If our church can ever get to the place where each member recognizes his or indispensability in the work of the whole, we will have achieved much of our reason for being.

Velma Ruch, *The Transforming Power of Prayer* Vol. 1, 135-146.

Have you had a sense of God's call to you? How did it come? What have you attempted to do with it? Are you aware that the calling of God to you is continuous and that your listening must be continuous as well? Are you flexible enough that you can change with circumstance and the direction of the call?

PRAYER: Dear God, we bow in humility before you when we recognize the many gifts you have bestowed upon us. May we never forget our first vow to follow you and in our lives fulfill your longing for us. Amen.

TUESDAY, THE SECOND WEEK OF LENT: "TEACH US TO PRAY"

SCRIPTURE: **Luke 11:1-2 Disciples' Question About Prayer**

He was praying in a certain place, and after he had finished one of his disciples said to him, "Lord, teach us to pray."

Matthew 6:5-14 Teaching on Prayer

"But whenever you pray, go into your room and shut the door and pray to your Father who is in secret; and your Father who sees in secret will reward you."

MEDITATION: The Prayer Life of Jesus

We discover that the prayer life of Jesus was not always serene, as neither is ours when we suffer, when we cannot see our way clearly, when we do not understand. But most of Jesus' prayers were of another type. They had to do with intimacy with the Father and with the needs of the disciples and by extension with our needs. We, too, can come to know the intimacy with our "Abba" that Jesus knew. This is so, as Paul reminded us, "because you are children, God has sent the Spirit of the Son into our hearts, crying, 'Abba! Father!" (Galatians 4:6).

...The Gospels are full of prayers of blessing, prayers of forgiveness and healing, and prayers concerned with the lost and downtrodden. The blessings of Jesus were both petitions and transference of grace. The prayer and answer to prayer were part of the same experience...

Velma Ruch, *The Transforming Power of Prayer*, Vol. 1, 38-39.

Jesus and Prayer

I am always impressed by the fact that it is recorded that the only thing that the disciples asked Jesus to teach them how to do was to pray. The references are many to his own constant dependence on prayer:

> *In the early morning, long before daylight, he got up and went away out to a lonely spot*
>
> (Mark 1:35).

> *After saying good-bye to them, he went up the hill to pray*
>
> (Mark 6:46).

> *Many crowds gathered to hear him...But he would withdraw to lonely places and pray.*
>
> (Luke 5:15, 16).

> *Now it happened that while he was praying by himself, his disciples were beside him. So he inquired of them, "Who do the crowds say that I am?"*
>
> (Luke 9:18)..

To Jesus, God breathed through all that is: the sparrow overcome by sudden death in its flight; the lily blossoming on the rocky hillside; the grass of the field and the clouds, light and burdenless or weighted down with unshed waters; the madman in chains or wandering among the barren rocks in the wastelands; the little baby in his mother's arms; the strutting insolence of the Roman Legion, the brazen queries of the tax collector; the children at play or old men quibbling in the market place; the august Sanhedrin fighting for its life amidst the arrogances of empire; the whisper of those who had forgotten Jerusalem, the great voiced utterance of the prophets who remembered – to Jesus, God breathed through all that is.

Howard Thurman, "Prayer," *Disciplines of the Spirit*
(Friends United Press, 1977) 88-89.

Growth in Prayer

Though prayer comes instinctively and almost naturally to us at certain points in our lives, growth in prayer is a lifetime endeavor. Teaching about prayer, Evelyn Underhill observed, is the teaching most needed in our time. In a time of upheaval and catastrophe of many kinds, there is a deep need for a well of vitality, a center of peace that can give us what the psalmist calls "truth in the inward being" (Psalm 51:6). In this sense, prayer is our most fundamental spiritual activity.

Velma Ruch, *The Transforming Power of Prayer*, Vol.1, 18.

Unceasing Prayer

When the Spirit has come to reside in someone, that person cannot stop praying; for the Spirit prays without ceasing in him. No matter if he is asleep or awake, prayer is going on in his heart all the time. He may be eating or drinking, he may be resting or working – the incense of prayer will ascend spontaneously from his heart. The slightest stirring of his heart is like a voice which sings in silence and in secret to the Invisible.

Isaac the Syrian. Quoted in Richard Foster, *Prayer*, 119.

"For the Christian, prayer is not simply an act but a lifestyle."

Anthony Chvala-Smith.

What has been your experience with prayer? Have you sensed a progression in your understanding? If so, how has that happened for you? What do you thirst to know and experience?

PRAYER: Our Father,
Who art in heaven,
Hallowed be thy name.
Thy kingdom come,
Thy will be done
On earth as it is done in heaven.
Give us this day our daily bread
And forgive us our trespasses
As we forgive those who trespass against us.
And suffer us not to be led into temptation
But deliver us from evil,
For thine is the kingdom and the power and the glory
Forever and ever. Amen.

(Matthew 6: 10-14 IV).

WEDNESDAY, THE SECOND WEEK OF LENT: LISTENING TO FOLLOW

SCRIPTURE: **1 Samuel 3 "Speak for Your Servant Is Listening"**

Now the Lord came and stood there, calling as before, "Samuel, Samuel!" And Samuel said, "Speak, Lord, for your servant is listening."

Isaiah 50:4-6 "He Wakens My Ear"

The Lord God has given me the tongue of a teacher, that I may know how to sustain the weary with a word. Morning by morning he wakens – wakens my ear to listen as those who are taught.

Doctrine and Covenants 162:1-2b Listen to Become

Listen, O people of the Restoration – you who would become a prophetic people…Listen to the voice that echoes across the eons of time and yet speaks anew in this moment. Listen to the voice, for it cannot be stilled, and it calls you once again to the great and marvelous work of building the peaceable kingdom, even Zion, on behalf of the One whose name you claim.

MEDITATION: Listening

We are living in a day, both in the church and in the world when it can no longer be business as usual. "If we are to make the spiritual discoveries that will save our age," Frank Lauback has written, "it will be in the direction Jesus took: intense, unwavering, daring obedience when God speaks – listening and saying yes at whatever cost." Are we equal to that? Are we committed enough to the pilgrim way to make the sacrifices that will allow us to be truly rooted and grounded in the love of our Lord and in the spiritual authority that will enflame and impassion us in our mission in the world? There is no question that is our call and our very reason for being. But whether we are prophets or disciples, true listening for the voice of the Lord will always involve the gift of discernment. With so many voices clamoring for a hearing and claiming to be spokespersons for the Divine, we need the ability to discern true spirits from false and be flexible enough not to compel the Lord to fit into our preconceived ideas. Such discernment requires both discrimination and openness to change.

Discernment is also a factor in listening to ourselves, in becoming more aware of who we are and why we respond as we do. Practicing discernment in our listening may mean we have a third ear that can hear the words that are spoken and what people are really saying behind them. Only in this way can we truly minister to their needs.

Listening as a spiritual discipline involves keeping the channels of communication with the Divine open. That does not happen accidentally. It means daily practice in sorting out that "still, small voice" from the many voices competing for our attention. It requires openness and a willingness to put our stubborn self-will on hold. It calls for discrimination in the emotions that assail us – discernment of spirits, it used to be called. Not every powerful experience is of divine origin. As a matter of fact, more often than not God speaks to us through the stillness, whispering gently to the receptive heart. It is prayer. It is grace. It is mystery. But having known God in the stillness, we can recognize that authentic voice when it thunders, as it will sometimes. True listening goes beyond communication to communion and we know that greatest of all gifts: living the Presence of our God. It is nourishment in the desert and a promise of flowering in the midst of the wilderness.

Velma Ruch, *Summoned to Pilgrimage*, 70-71

Have you learned to discriminate between God's voice and the many other voices calling to you including your own will and desires? How is your sense of touch? Can you recognize the touch of God even if it is "as light as the touch of a butterfly's wing"? Are you ever deaf to the word of God even if it thunders?

PRAYER: Listening God, you have told us that before we call, you will answer and while we are yet speaking you will hear. May we in like manner engage in the silence that will allow us to hear your voice, even the slightest whisper and follow where it calls. Amen.

THURSDAY, THE SECOND WEEK OF LENT: JESUS' INAUGURAL STATEMENT

SCRIPTURE: **Luke 4:16-21 Jesus Reading from the Scroll**

"The Spirit of the Lord is upon me, because he has anointed me to bring good news to the poor."

MEDITATION: The Anointed Life

What did Jesus mean by the words, "because the Lord has anointed me"? What specific meaning can be affirmed when Jesus said, "The Spirit of the Lord is upon me because he has anointed me"? In general, the verb "to anoint" by biblical definition means to pour, rub, or to spread, as an ointment, an oil, or fragrance...But the basic idea is that when this special ointment was used, something significant happened. In most cases the basic intent symbolizes and concretizes divine authorization, within religious ritual. It gives evidence of the impartation of wisdom and knowledge and the communication of the grace and power of God. Such persons who were so anointed, by virtue of their anointing, were expected to serve as representatives of God in whose name and power they were so anointed.

James A. Forbes, *The Holy Spirit and Preaching*
(Abingdon Press, 1989), 27-28.

The anointing of the Holy Spirit is that process by which one comes to a fundamental awareness of God's appointment, empowerment, and guidance for the vocation to which we are called as the body of Christ. It is that process that leads us to yield fully to the revealed will of God.

Forbes, 37

Given the challenges of the secular age, can we continue to talk about our own sense of empowerment and authorization in isolation? The task of calling the church and the age to revitalized spirituality is such that we cannot do it alone. The challenge before the church is to find a way for all of its members to talk together about the anointing of the Spirit and to seek the depth of experience to which it points.

Forbes, 39

The Spirit–Embodied Life

The anointing of which Jesus spoke will always be a mark of Spirit presence. "You shall receive power when the Holy Spirit has come upon you," Jesus told his disciples before his ascension. That is anointing. Anointing is an act of consecration for work to be done. And as practiced by the Hebrew, it was thought to confer upon the anointed one a special endowment of the Spirit. Anointing not only requires specific response from the recipient but promises increased power in the performance of the calling. How do we recognize the time or times of anointing in our lives? How did Jesus know at his baptism that the time for which he had been waiting had come? How has the calling and anointing come to you? How did you know, in the terminology of James Forbes, that it was launch time, that it was time to move out of the ready room to the full consecration of your life to the mission of Jesus Christ? Perhaps for you it was not a one-time event only, for anointing is in the process just as Zion is in the process, not just in the end product. Jesus said, "I have yet many things to say to you, but you cannot bear them now." About this James Forbes comments, "I like to think of the Spirit the way Jesus has characterized it. According to this text, the Spirit becomes a director of continuing education for our spirits. We are not beginners. This is not kindergarten. We are already on the way. But the Spirit that brought us this far continues to direct our paths...The director who has been with us all the way, is standing right there with us. We are not in the ministers' workshop alone. The Spirit is there with us." (79-80).

In what language has the Spirit anointed you to speak? That language is by no means limited to spoken words. Are you anointed with the language of presence? Do you have the spirit of discernment that can hear the cries from the dark even when they cannot be expressed? Do you have the gift of intercessory prayer so that your spiritual weight can open another channel for the afflicted and broken-hearted to the Divine? Are you anointed with the gift of hospitable space so you are not threatened by the actions or beliefs of others but can enfold them in accepting love and to allow them to blossom into the people they are capable of becoming? Are you anointed with the gift of stirring speech or with serving or with participating in acts of mercy? For all of us the possibility of this kind of anointing exists. No one is excluded, neither priesthood nor member. All are called according to the gifts of God unto them and in response to that call are endowed with power.

Velma Ruch

What Is the Spirit?

What is this Spirit that has so much power and what did Christ mean when at the beginning of his active ministry he read from Isaiah, "The Spirit of the Lord is upon me"? Though many responses can be given to this question, the final answer is that the Spirit is God. It is God present in our lives and active in the world. It is the self-revealing and self-giving God of which Christ was also the manifestation. The Spirit witnesses to the divinity of Christ and is an extension of his ministry. Christ's physical presence was transformed into spiritual presence and continues his redemptive work in our lives.

Velma Ruch, "Sensing the Leading of My Spirit," *Herald*, September, 1995, 7.

PRAYER:

Touch me, Lord, with thy Spirit eternal;
Stir my soul to respond to thy call.
Take my love, for I offer it freely;
Hear my prayer as I thank thee for all.

Teach me. Lord, to walk humbly before thee;
May I hasten thy will to obey.
Make me wise to see clearly thy purpose;
Keep me true to my calling I pray.

Fill me, Lord, with thine infinite power;
Make me firm, make me pure, make me whole.
With thy Spirit to strengthen and guide me,
I shall serve thee with all of my soul.

Adapted from the Russian by Don C. Rawson.
Hymns of the Saints, # 409.

FRIDAY, THE SECOND WEEK OF LENT: THE LIVING WATER

SCRIPTURE: **John 4:1-30 The Woman at the Well**

"If you knew the gift of God, and who it is that is saying to you, 'Give me a drink,' you would have asked him, and he would have given you living water."

MEDITATION: **Prayer of the Beggar**

Lord, hear me, I am ancestor
to the woman at the well,
earthen jar to fill.
I am your beggar
set out for the day,
bowl in hand,
open to your will.

Day after day I have gone
in search of water
returning with only the salt
from tears
as token of the day.

Now I drink my fill
of your Living Water.
my thirst is quenched!
I lift this humble vessel
to the Heavens
in thanksgiving
and pass it on.
Amen.

Phyllis Price, *Holy Fire* (Paulist Press 1998), 46.

Behold the Waters How They Flow

Elbert A. Smith in an early poem expressed so simply and powerfully the invitation extended to us to stoop down and drink from that life-giving water:

Behold the waters, how they flow,
The waters of eternal life,
As silently they come and go,
Within their healing depths no woe,
Stoop down, stoop low,
And drink, and go
Declare the message to and fro
That all mankind may come and know
The waters of eternal life.

That same invitation was extended at the end of the book of Revelation:

The Spirit and the bride say, "Come.""
And let everyone who hears say, "Come."
Let anyone who wishes take the water.
Of life as a gift.

(Rev. 22:17)
Velma Ruch *Summoned to Pilgrimage*, 133.

Come to the Water

Come all you who are thirsty,
Come to the sources of living water
Some of us feel flooded. There is too much to do and
we feel in danger of going under.
Come, rest beside the still waters and feel the ease of the cool stream
Some of us feel empty. We give and pour ourselves out
with no time to tap into the source
Come, taste the eternal springs of living water. Drink deep and long
Some of us feel blocked and stagnant. Judgment,
denial, frustration and wounds limit the flow of peace.
Come, be plunged deep into the healing waters and fresh rivers
of God's love
We come to touch the living water and remember our baptism.
Let the joyful water flow.

Larry J. Peacock, *Alive Now*, (May/June, 1994), 5.

The Day After: The Challenge of Living Water

We don't know what happened to the Samaritan woman when she began the serious searching of her life after those two dramatic days with Jesus. Now she still had to return to the home from which she had come. The same problems she had known before were still there. Some of the demeaning experiences and abuse she might have undergone were still part of her memory. Some of the desires that may have trapped her in the first place were still there. Though many in the community may perhaps have changed their opinion of her, many had not. Would they accept her without distrust? She had through Jesus found a source of healing. Without that encounter no genuine change was likely to take place, but she was still wounded. In spite of the tremendous joy she felt in recognizing Jesus, he had touched the wounded part of her life and it was still painful. The Spirit does that It is a significant part of the healing process. As Helen Bruch Pearson has written so powerfully,

Once we have experienced living water, we make ourselves vulnerable. We risk leaving behind the old container that held what had kept us bound. And we go. While we may be called to go into situations and places that are foreign and strange, we are also sent back to familiar situations and circumstances where we have received hurt and rejection. Regardless of the place or time, we are vessels of salvation and reconciliation. We do not decide who is thirsty and in need of living water. The gift we have been given is for the benefit of all who thirst. For them we pour out what we have been given. Like the Samaritan woman we are haulers of living water.

Do What You Have the Power to Do
(Upper Room Books, 1992). 159-160.

We are always confronted with a double call: Transformation and Mission. The question is, How do we get from here to there? How do we live out the challenges with which living water confronts us?

Velma Ruch

Why are you thirsty? What spiritual needs do you have that you desire to be quenched by living water? Do you have living water to give to those who thirst?

PRAYER: God of Love and Truth, you have aroused a thirst in us and we, like the woman at the well, pray, "Give us of that water." By giving, you make us ask and over and over we have been blessed by your living water. May we ever come to drink at the well of salvation. Amen.

SATURDAY, THE SECOND WEEK OF LENT: BEING FORMED FOR MINISTRY

SCRIPTURE: **II Timothy 1:7,9,13-14; 2:1-3, 14-16, 22-25 Paul's Advice**

Hold to the standard of sound teaching that you have heard from me, in the faith and love that are in Christ Jesus. Guard the good treasure that is entrusted to you with the help of the Holy Spirit living in us.

Book of Mormon, Alma 15:51-69 Called to Be an Instrument of God

And this is my glory, that perhaps I may be an instrument in the hands of God to bring some soul to repentance; and this is my joy.

Doctrine and Covenants Section 11:4 Assisting in the Work

...and no one can assist in this work, except he shall be humble and full of love, having faith, hope, and charity, being temperate in all things whatsoever shall be entrusted to his care.

Doctrine and Covenants Section 85:21 That You May Be Prepared

...that ye may be prepared in all things when I shall send you again, to magnify the calling whereunto I have called you, and the mission with which I have commissioned you.

MEDITATION: Chosen, Called, and Commissioned by Christ

Our view of ourselves as disciples who have been personally chosen by Jesus should alter our whole attitude toward him and motivate us strongly for the work which has been given us to do....The church today suffers because so many of its members feel they have somehow made the decision to join the church and follow Christ, rather than

having a sense of being chosen. But it is only as we see ourselves chosen, called and commissioned by Christ to be his disciples that we will want to stretch ourselves –make every effort to do whatever is required –even present our bodies a living sacrifice holy and acceptable to God to accomplish the tasks that have been given to us.

Wallace B. Smith, "International Perspectives on the Temple,"
International Leadership Conference, 1988.

Let the Words of My Mouth

In her book In God's Presence Marjorie Hewitt Suchocki asks the question, "What is God's native tongue?' The answer is "Each of them, of course – and none of them." None of them because "God hears from a place deeper than language." She writes,

Perhaps every language is translated back into God's language of the Spirit . . . Because of this deeper than language communication, the clumsiest prayers in our native speech, translated by God, may be offerings of sheer beauty in the poetry of the Spirit.(39)

Velma Ruch, *The Transforming Power of Prayer*, Vol. 2, 135.

Speaking the Language of the Heart

To learn to recognize and speak the language of the heart is a vital human need. If such language is not available to us, part of our inner life will shrivel. Many of the difficulties in the world today are the result of our inability to express our inner longings and give them a name. We can readily communicate facts and scientific data, but feelings are a different matter. Poets have done it, and we can learn from them the words in which such feelings can be released. They teach us, as Arthur Oakman once expressed it, "to take the words soiled by human intercourse and make them tell the truth." We learn the art, as another writer described it, of "the finer accommodation of speech to the vision within" (Walter Pater). If we do not learn to respond to and speak this language, our souls become parched, and we settle for the mediocre in thought and life, unaware that there are far richer forms of expression to give reality to that which stirs uncreated within us.

Distinguished Author Lectures, 1988-1989, Velma Ruch,
"My Heart Was Full," 55.

Study to Show Thyself Approved

The purpose of the spiritual disciplines is transformation of life, freedom from those things that hold us down and inhibit the new creation which God desires from us. If study is to be called a spiritual discipline, the knowledge acquired must be related to being. The difference in study generally and study as a spiritual discipline is not in the material studied but how it is studied. Without relationship to being it becomes what Theodore Roethke called "the stupor of knowledge lacking inwardness," or as Milton said it, we can be "deep verst in books and shallow in ourselves." The scriptures say it is possible "to learn and learn and not come to a knowledge of the truth." Kierkegaard perhaps said it most memorably when he referred to those "who think in a palace and live in a doghouse." What all of this says is that we need to relate a technique of investigation to an account of being.

Part of our spiritual heritage in the Restoration movement is the strong emphasis on study as a spiritual discipline. It was not called that but this is what is meant by "Seek learning by study and also by faith." It was a recognition that if ministry was to speak to the needs of the world, to have impact on individuals and social structures, it needed to be a competent ministry, one that had sought learning by study and by faith. Section 85 reminds us that there is no limit to the areas we may choose to investigate. This is so, the statement continues, in order that we "may be prepared in all things when I shall send you again, to magnify the calling where unto I have called you, and the mission with which I have commissioned you."

Velma Ruch "The Discipline of Study,"
The Order of Evangelists Training Resource, 103.

Are You Aware of God's Design for Your Life?

"You have not chosen me, but I have chosen you, and ordained you that you should go and bring forth fruit, and that your fruit should remain." (John 15:16) Are you aware of God's design for your life? Ask God to help you write a life mission statement, whether you're in the early stages of your life or you have many years behind you. What did God have in mind for you when your body was still being formed? How is God forming you spiritually now? Who does God want you to become? What are your dreams, your goals, your special abilities, your spiritual gifts? How does God want to use them? Dare to pray boldly. Dare to dream boldly

The Spiritual Formation Bible, NIV, 817.

PRAYER: Gracious God, deep in our hearts, whether we immediately recognized it or not, we have been aware of your call. That awareness has caused a hunger in our lives to know you more fully and to serve you with greater competence. We truly wish to be men and women who serve you with humility and love. Empower us with your Spirit as we move forward in trust. Amen

THE THIRD WEEK OF LENT
THEME: A GREAT AND MARVELOUS WORK

SUNDAY, THE THIRD WEEK OF LENT: COMMUNITY

SCRIPTURE: **Acts 1:12-14; 2:1-4 Community of Prayer**

When the day of Pentecost had come, they were all together in one place. And suddenly from heaven there came a sound like the rush of a violent wind, and it filled the entire house where they were sitting.

Acts 4:23-31 The Believers Pray for Boldness

When they had prayed, the place in which they were gathered together was shaken; and they were all filled with the Holy Spirit and spoke the word of God with boldness.

Matthew 18:18-20 Where Two or Three Are Gathered

For where two or three are gathered in my name, I am there among them.

MEDITATION: The Centrality of Community

Christianity is not a religion of individual achievement. From the start of his ministry, Jesus highlighted the centrality of community to his message and taught that the life of fellowship was essential to discipleship. Jesus called, prepared, and empowered not separate individuals, but a group of women and men to be the nucleus of God's renewing grace in and for the world. They stumblingly followed him, endured the devastation of his death, were reclaimed by the miracle of Easter, and sent into all the world in the power of the Spirit. Jesus knew that following him could never be a solo performance; thus he taught the disciples to pray not "my Father" but "our Father, who art in heaven." He promised them that in the future he always would be present in their midst when they gathered in his name (Matthew 18:20). At his last meal he told all of the disciples to drink from the cup, not just one or two, and he declared that his death would be for the many, not for the few (Matthew 26:27-28) And after Easter, it was in breaking bread together that his followers found renewed confirmation of his risen presence.

By planting the seed that became the church, Jesus revealed that the renewal of our humanity would not be found apart from life in the company of those who trust in him. The church is not an afterthought to the good news; it is integral to the good news.

Anthony Chvala-Smith in
Understanding the Way: Exploring Our Christian Faith
(Herald House, 2003), 41-42.

Prayerful Approach to Pain

Pain is a natural part of communal life. At times it is the fierce pain of loss or sickness, another's or our own. It is the half-comic pain of personalities that are bound to rub against one another, no matter how many years they have occupied the same space. It is the draining pain of divisions that will not fade away.

The response to pain in the community of faith is often something less than prayer. It is busy avoidance...or an agreed-upon silence...or the sincere desire to be of aid that, each time it arises, ultimately bows to feelings that say, "Others can handle this more adequately than I; it is best that I stand aside."

The prayerful approach to pain in the community of faith is both personal and corporate. The prayerful approach lets me grant that by myself I cannot treat the pain. Similarly, it allows those of us in community to acknowledge that we cannot fully assuage the pain even when we all work together. In the prayerful approach to pain we turn outward. We open to the One whose compassion completes our finite efforts to be of aid. We welcome the One whose wisdom can encourage and season our own imperfect speech. In essence, we allow the divine power to flow even into the places of our greatest weakness.

Stephen V. Doughty, "Why are they, well, so...?!"
Weavings (May/June, 1999), 41.

Open Your Hearts

Open your hearts and feel the yearnings of your brothers and sisters who are lonely, despised, fearful, neglected, unloved. Reach out in understanding, clasp their hands, and invite all to share in the blessings of community created in the name of the One who suffered on behalf of all.

Do not be fearful of one another. Respect each life journey, even in its brokenness and uncertainty, for each person has walked alone at times. Be ready to listen and slow to criticize, lest judgments be unrighteous and unredemptive..

Be patient with one another, for creating sacred community is arduous and even painful. But it is to loving community such as this that each is called. Be courageous and visionary, believing in the power of just a few vibrant witnesses to transform the world. Be assured that love will overcome the voices of fear, division and deceit.

Doctrine and Covenants, Section 161: 3a,b,c.

Telling Our Stories

The community...offers a context for relationships. Relation with other journeyers provide support for struggles, offer the energy for which the kingdom of God calls, and serve as a corrective for the interpretation of the presence of the holy God in human history. In the community, also, persons tell their stories. The hearers clarify the meaning of the tale, they affirm, correct and help the storytellers relate their stories to the story. The faith community spreads the master narrative like a canopy, and its shadow forms the superstructure of individual stories. Without the larger story, personal narratives lack coherence, direction and ultimate meaning.

Ben Campbell Johnson, *Pastoral Spirituality*,
(The Westminster Press, 1988) 29.

How is your story related to the larger story? What impact has community had on your life, both inside the church and out?

PRAYER: Living God, it is in community that we come to know you as we share your love with one another. May we always be aware of those whose space we share in the world and live with them in righteousness and peace. Amen.

MONDAY, THE THIRD WEEK OF LENT: THE BODY OF CHRIST

SCRIPTURE: **I Cor. 12:12-27 One Body with Many Members**

For in the one Spirit we were all baptized into one body – Jews or Greeks, slaves or free – and we were made to drink of one Spirit.

MEDITATION: **A Prayer of Unity**

Dear Lord,
as you called the lame man to walk,
the blind one to see,
so are we called to be
the one body of your people,
the whole composed in equal parts
of all colors, cultures and tongues....
Thus are we called to gather our weaknesses
that one might complement another,
that each dark one might illuminate
a darker one still
until together
we are rendered light.

In center soul are we called
to reconcile differences
through empathy and compassion,
through the experience of another's pain
felt as our own.
Quiet our tongues and thoughts
that with the heart
we may listen.

Call us to gather in celebration
of victories large and small
of one another,
to join hands at last
in a circle of love,
united in the community
you would have us be. Amen.

Phyllis Price, *Holy Fire* (Paulist Press)

Corporate Expression of the Spirit

The body of Christ witnesses to the corporate expression of the Spirit. Use of the Spirit just for individual satisfaction and inner peace is a betrayal of its intended function. The call of the Spirit is to community. We are called to be a people, a bonded, caring community, what has been called "a social creation of grace." The Spirit thus working among us can free us from doctrinal blinders, from willful self-interest, from deafness and near-sightedness. Our vision becomes immensely improved and we are enabled to see with new eyes the truths that were always waiting for our comprehension. It is in community, I believe, that many of those truths will emerge. It is there we lend out our minds to one another. It is there we come to a recognition of needs both expressed and unexpressed. It is there our vision becomes widened to take in those far and near in need of justice, peace, and love. It is there the Spirit works among us

We have much yet to learn about the corporate expression of the Spirit. Though our church in its emphasis on Spirit guidance, on present-day revelation, on theocratic democracy, on consensus building, on "all are called" has given us much to work with, many of the truths involved are yet undiscovered. Can we as a church in this moment of our history not only make a contribution in regard to the working of the Spirit with individuals but also in and through the corporate body? We are in great need of this understanding not just for ourselves, but for ministry to all those who search for the expression of God's will in community. It is basic to our dream of Zion.

Velma Ruch, "Sensing the Leading of My Spirit,"
Herald, September, 1995, 8

Community

"Team games are compulsory in the school of Divine Love," Evelyn Underhill has written. "There must be no getting in a corner with a nice spiritual book." She did not object to "nice spiritual books" –she wrote at least forty of them herself. What she is saying is that spiritual books by themselves will not help us much unless we use them in "team games," working with others.....We need the transformation that comes from the times spent "in the closet," in private worship, but we need the community to help us achieve a coherence between the inner and the outer, how we can relate the best of who we are to the group....

As Robert Mulholland has observed, "Our unique individuality is one of the gifts we bring to the body of Christ....The diversity in our temperament types is part of the glorious diversity of the body of Christ in which God nurtures us to wholeness" (*Invitaion to a Journey*, 144). It is easy for us to assent to such a statement in regard to ourselves, but how difficult it is for us to accept the uniqueness of others with the same grace.

Once we realize we are all 'cells" in the body of Christ we recognize that neither the body nor we can exist without a genuine corporate relationship. We see out of different windows. We understand differently; our knowledge is in different area. Alone our vision is imperfect. To "see with new eyes" we must have a corporate vision in which we help one another to overcome biases, to be led into new ways of thinking, to break out of narrow mindedness, to avoid putting God in a box, *our box*.

We have spoken of the community's need for us. That has often meant specifically the congregation, the body of Christ. But that is not enough. We must reach beyond that small group to the larger world community. Sometimes we don't want to. Part of the appeal of cults is promised safety for their own adherents. At one time that was true of the Community of Christ as well. I believe we moved out of the cult mentality when we saw that the welfare of the world was more important than our own safety. We have learned how important it is that the message of the gospel reach a world in disarray, hungering and thirsting for what will give coherence and meaning to life. But it has to begin with individual transformation and community transformation. What that means is that we have reconciling responsibility not just to ourselves but to the church community of which we are a part...

Our lives are linked with other lives. How important it is for those who, as it says in Ephesians, have been "without Christ...having no hope and without God in the world" to find that hope and to be invited in. It is the joy of no longer being an outsider kept out by dividing walls of hostility. It is the assurance that they are "no longer strangers and aliens" but they are now "members of the household of God" (see Ephesians 2:12-19). We are all included in the divine embrace, both the far and the near, those who have denied and those who have accepted. We can all be included in the warmth of fellowship of the love of Christ in the household of God. Because this is true, :let all of us speak he truth to our neighbors" (Ephesians 4:25).

Velma Ruch,_*The Transforming Power of Prayer,* Vol. 2, 113-123.

How has community functioned in your life in the church and out? What good things in your life do you attribute to community?

PRAYER: We are so deeply grateful, O God, that you have invited us in to be part of your fellowship of love. We are not only uplifted and sustained by your love but also the love of our brothers and sisters and the great communion of saints who walk with us in the Spirit. We wish to be an integral part of that community giving of ourselves in love and service as we respond to your invitation to us. Amen.

TUESDAY, THE THIRD WEEK OF LENT: A GREAT AND MARVELOUS WORK

SCRIPTURE: **Doctrine and Covenants 4 The Gift of the Restoration**

Now, behold, a marvelous work is about to come forth among the children of men, therefore, O ye that embark in the service of God, see that ye serve him with all your heart, might, mind, and strength that ye may stand blameless before God at the last day.

Doctrine and Covenants 10:1-3 The Field is White

Behold, the field is white already to harvest, therefore, whoso desireth to reap, let him thrust in his sickle with his might and reap while the day lasts

Doctrine and Covenants 156:5 a-c The Life and Ministry of the Redeemer of the World

And it shall be a place in which the essential meaning of the Restoration as healing and redeeming agent is given new life and understanding, inspired by the life and witness of the Redeemer of the world.

MEDITATION: In the Grove

As we enter the Temple reception hall, we see a double door framed by sculptured, engraved glass. The representation is of the grove near Palmyra, New York, where the young Joseph Smith experienced his transforming vision. The entry not only represents the point of origin that led to the formation of the church but it affirms the reality of the Divine/human encounter and emphasized our belief that as human beings we are created for such encounter.

The experience of the young boy, Joseph, which led to his time of spiritual awakening, can teach us much. He had just entered his teens and like all teenagers was searching to discover his own identity. It was a time of great religious ferment with a multitude of voices clamoring to be heard. Joseph already sensed that behind these voices was a significance he could not afford to ignore. He could not make sense of all he heard and find a voice that rang true to him. His confusion grew and he turned to the scriptures for help. There he came upon a statement in James 1:5, "If any of you lack wisdom, let him ask of God." The passage came alive to him. It seemed to be a point of direction. But "asking of God," how does one do that? He was inexperienced in prayer, but in his great need thought he "might venture."

Joseph went to the grove alone and there opened himself in prayer. He was no doubt stunned by what happened next. Instead of help, he experienced "great darkness" and struggled within himself for survival. But then, as he writes, "at this moment of great alarm I saw a pillar of light exactly over my head, above the brightness of the sun, which descended gradually until it fell upon me. It no sooner appeared that I found myself delivered from the enemy that held me bound." It was then two personages appeared in a vision and he heard one say, "This is my beloved Son, hear him." Now he knew that the voice he must heed was the voice of Christ. He dedicated himself to obedience and faithful listening and in the process changed the religious history of the world.

Velma Ruch, *Summoned to Pilgrimage*
(Herald Publishing House, 1994) 44-45.

Mission Statement

We proclaim Jesus Christ and promote communities of joy, hope, love, and peace.

A Covenant Community

The church's reason for existence is mission: to proclaim Jesus Christ and to promote communities of joy, hope, peace, and love. That mission has two centers of activity:

(1) nurture within the covenant community, the body of Christ, the church, the congregation and

(2) ministry to the world at large.

But we cannot be a viable force to the larger community unless the word goes out from a covenant community that in every aspect of its ministry proclaims the endowing presence of the ever-living Christ. Our challenge both individually and as a group is to proclaim in life and word the gospel of Christ and its relevance for all.

The Dream

What is it that causes members of the Reorganized Church of Jesus Christ of Latter Day Saints [The Community of Christ] to support a religion so distinctive? Why are members willing to sacrifice in so many ways to worship with the Saints in small groups, often remotely located at great distances from their homes? How do these dedicated people manage to withstand the misunderstanding, the questions, the differences in lifestyle, and the temptation to go to the large, popular churches that seem to offer everything for everyone?

The answer for most lies in the dream of Zion, a people of one heart and one mind, empowered by the Holy Spirit,...a Spiritual Awakening. The cause of Zion inspires the people of God!

Brochure: *The Temple: Ensign of Peace*

A Willingness To Be Stretched

Vital communities of faith allow themselves to be stretched by the Holy Spirit. They permit an expansion that they would never think up on their own. This states the matter somewhat abstractly, but the stretching itself is forever specific. The issues posed to the earliest faith communities were crisp and unexpected. Do we let the Gentiles join us? Do we speak boldly of what we have seen in Christ Jesus? Do we embrace a vision of power based not on coercion and the amassing of goods but on service and simplicity? The Yes that the Holy Spirit urged in response to these questions radically redrew the boundaries of communal experience. And the communities that allowed that Yes to breathe through them found themselves in uncharted and often hostile territory.

The Holy Spirit has never ceased attempting to recast who we are and how we live in our communities of faith. The spirit comes from the realm of utter wholeness and perpetually seeks to draw us there. So the questions continue. Do we welcome all who seek the living God, or is the boundary of our love tight, confined to those whose views, backgrounds, and enthusiasms mirror our own? Do we honestly probe the gift of our faith and openly speak it, or is this gift, little visited and seldom spoken, growing distant even from ourselves? Is our collective way of living such that persons notice any difference at all when they look at us?

To say that vital faith communities allow themselves to be stretched by the Holy Spirit is not to imply the stretching is easy. The early church hotly debated what to do about the Gentiles. The congregation near my home that joined the civil rights movement nearly split.

The process is often rough, the path to clarity long and torturous. Nonetheless, however raucous and painful the stretching may be, it is the steady opening to the Spirit's breath, and breadth, that allows fresh life to surge within us. And it is the stretched community that most fully conveys the vibrant power of God's love.

Stephen V. Doughty, "Why are they, well, so…?!"
Weavings (May/June, 1999) 39-40.

We Limit Not the Truth of God

A favorite hymn in the Community of Christ is "We Limit Not the Truth of God" (Hymns of the Saints, 309) Its refrain expresses one of our deepest convictions: "The Lord hath yet more light and truth to break forth from his word." On his last night with his disciples, Jesus made a promise to them. He said, "I still have many things to say to you , but you cannot bear them now. When the Spirit of truth comes, he will guide you into all the truth (John 16:12-13) Jesus was telling the disciples that they didn't know it all, that the kind of truth he represents can be grasped only as it unfolds. It has been tempting for Christians to suppose that the truth of the gospel could be frozen and fixed for all time in certain words or forms. This has not been our approach. The truth of the gospel is alive: it is not a list, an institution, a system of ideas or even a book, but a person. The Risen Lord is present by the Spirit to guide us ever onward in the Way. That means that we expect to change – both as individual disciples and as a community. Until the Word, through whom God speaks, comes again in glory, nothing can be considered finished, nothing settled, nothing perfect, nothing complete. And so we walk on.

Anthony Chvala-Smith, *Understanding the Way*
(Herald House, 2003) 63-64.

What are the tap roots of your faith? What is it that holds you to the church of which you are a member?

PRAYER: Great and marvelous are thy works, O Lord of hosts, almighty One!
Earth and firmament speak thy praise, Thy name is written in the sun.

Thou hast fashioned with thine own hand The earth below, the heavens above;
Oh, how wonderful is thy power, And yet how tender is thy love.

O thou infinite, living God, Upon us now thy Spirit pour.
We would worship thee laud and praise Thy holy name forever more,
Amen

Charlotte G. Homer, *Hymns of the Saints,* # 48.

WEDNESDAY, THE THIRD WEEK OF LENT: GOD'S REVELATORY PRESENCE

SCRIPTURE: **Book of Mormon, 2 Nephi 12:63-65 Other Words Yet To Be Spoken**

And because I have spoken one word, ye need not suppose that I cannot speak another; for my work is not yet finished; neither shall it be until the end of man; neither from that time henceforth forever.

Book of Mormon, Jacob 3:9-13 Despise Not the Revelations of God

How unsearchable are the depths of the mysteries of him; and it is impossible that man should find out all his ways. No man knows of his ways save it be revealed to him; wherefore, brethren, despise not the revelations of God.

Acts 9:1-19 The Conversion of Saul

Now as Saul was going along and approaching Damascus suddenly a light from heaven flashed around him. He fell to the ground and heard a voice saying to him, "Saul, Saul, why do you persecute me?"

MEDITATION: God's Revelatory Presence

The mystics and prophets of all times and religions have borne testimony of God's revelatory presence. Most of us tend to dissociate ourselves from the word "mystic." We see it as something esoteric from which we wish to keep our distance. But we can't call ourselves a prophetic people without affirming the invasive power of a self-revealing God. That designation makes mystics-in-training of us all. The Quaker, Rufus Jones, has written,

> Mysticism in its broadest meaning is a type of religion which puts its emphasis on immediate awareness of the soul's relation with God, a direct and immediate consciousness of Divine Presence. It feels like an invasion, like a thrust from beyond the mind of the individual – something breaks in on the mind, one is met in the way, and it feels like the Life of God breaking in on the soul. The experience clarifies life, gives it direction, marching power, emotional intensity....The recipients in all instances are stung awake and sent beyond themselves.
>
> Rufus Jones, *The Radiant Life* (The Macmillan Company, 1951) 95.

Many prophets and saints and ordinary people of past and present have given testimony to the reality of this experience. It happened to Isaiah in the temple whose lips were touched with fire; to Ezekiel who in a vision of fire was commanded to stand upon his feet so God could speak to him; to Jeremiah who could not give up his prophetic task because of the fire burning in his bones, to Paul on the road to Damascus when he was blinded by the light of Christ, to Samuel who heard the voice in the temple, to young Joseph as he knelt in the grove, to Mary confronted by the angel Gabriel; to Esther who came to the kingdom for such a time as this, to Enos who "hungered" for divine presence, to the brother of Jared as related in the story of the Jaredites in the Book of Mormon, and on and on. Though each responded in different ways according to the situation in which they found themselves, for all of them it was an experience of sanctification, refining fire, and of life direction, a vocation.

Though the Spirit comes to all of us in varying intensity we recognize by our burning heart that God is calling us to the fulfillment of some task. We feel on the verge of an understanding for which some expression is required, whether it is taking up anew a task we were about to desert, or finding the words God needs to have spoken, or challenging us to further sanctification of our lives, or whatever else God may desire of us. For us to be called a prophetic people means that not only do we need to be open to this experience individually but also recognize its presence "where two or three are gathered together."

Velma Ruch, "The Church of Burning Hearts" (unpublished)

The Invasion of the Holy Spirit

God's immanent presence in us is truly a wonder. It is the signature of God written upon our hearts. It opens our hearts and minds to the beautiful within and without. But it also establishes a deep longing to meet the author of the signature. Sensing presence through nature, through the beautiful, creates in us a thirst for something more. What we have experienced, as C. S. Lewis has observed, is "only the scent of a flower we have not found, the echo of a tune we have not heard, news from a country we have never visited." A desire is built in us for a Presence that can deal with us personally, that intersects with our spirits and to whom we can speak or simply rest in enveloping love. It is the experience of the Divine Other. What we long for is the direct invasion of the Holy Spirit, that Comforter that Jesus promised his disciples would soon be theirs. They had the experience on Pentecost and were transformed into a prophetic people. "I had my face to the things enlightened and my back to the Light" wrote Augustine in describing his long road to conversion. Conversion will ever require the turning around, the facing of the Light itself, sanctification, and the saying "yes" to the most important question that will ever come to us.

Velma Ruch

God First Sought Us

Revelation is not a human action, but a divine one. Revelation happened because God first sought us, not because humans first sought God. Apart from the gracious, self-giving acts in which God has come to us, we really would be in the dark. But because of revelation, we know ourselves to be creatures beloved of God, not orphans in an empty universe. Because of revelation, we have come to know the very One who is the Author of all life. That is why the authors of scripture, who first experienced God's mighty acts, responded in song and confession: "Sing praises to him [God], tell of all his wonderful works (Psalm 105); we have seen it and testify to it" (1 John 1).

Anthony Chvala –Smith in *Understanding the Way,* 14.

I Sought the Lord

I sought the Lord, and afterward I knew
He moved my soul to seek him, seeking me;
It was not I that found, O Savior, true;
No, I was found of thee.

Thou didst reach forth thy hand and mine enfold;
I walked and sank not on the storm-vexed sea;
'Twas not so much that I on thee took hold
As thou, dear Lord, on me.

I find, I walk, I love, but oh, the whole
Of love is but my answer, Lord, to thee!
For thou were long beforehand with my soul;
Always thou didst love me.

Anonymous, *Hymns of the Saints,* # 213.

Continuing Revelation

The Community of Christ believes that the Sacred Story is not finished yet. There are chapters yet to be written and we are invited to let ourselves become part of that process. From the time of the first followers of Jesus through the long centuries until today, the meaning of God's revelation in Jesus Christ has been continuously unfolding. Hence we speak of *continuing revelation.* Wherever God's activity is faithfully proclaimed and received, people begin to see themselves differently: as connected with all creation, as those who are loved, forgiven, and called to play their own small but vital part in the Sacred Story.

Anthony Chvala-Smith, *ibid.,* 15.

"Perhaps the most fundamental and central theological concept of the Restoration movement is the belief in divine revelation."

Alan Tyree

The Prophetic Spirit Is Not Dead

People today customarily dismiss the direct speech of God to human ears. . . . Yet I firmly believe that the prophetic spirit has not died, nor has it ceased to speak. . . There are still prophets among us. I believe there are professors with whom I teach that are prophetic; there are pastors of congregations who have the gift of prophecy; among the laity, gifts of prophecy often reveal themselves in committee meetings, classes and private conversation. Living before God means listening for prophetic speech and becoming attentive to the word of God that comes to us through another.

Ben Campbell Johnson, *Living Before God: Deepening Our Sense of Divine Presence* (Grand Rapids, Michigan:William B. Eerdmans Publishing Co.), 64.

What does the word "prophetic" mean to you? Do you recognize the prophetic even in unexpected places? How would you define "a prophetic people"? Alan Tyree calls the belief in divine revelation "perhaps the most fundamental and central theological concept of the Restoration." Do you agree?

PRAYER: **FOUNTAIN OF ALL REVELATION**

Fountain of all revelation, Grant us thy life-giving power.
Without thee no sure salvation Will deliver us this hour.
May no veil of our tradition Mask the light that comes from thee!
Let not pride nor low ambition Waste the strength that sets us free.

God, our rock of revelation, We would build our lives on thee;
For without thy sure foundation None can find stability.
We will order not thy wisdom To some cherished form or mold,
But will search for truths now hidden As we live by those we hold.

Deam Ferris, *Hymns of the Saints,* # 298.

THURSDAY, THE THIRD WEEK OF LENT: STANDING FAST

SCRIPTURE: **Psalm 57:7-11 My Heart Is Steadfast**

My heart is steadfast, O God, my heart is steadfast I will sing and make melody.

Lamentations 3: 19-26 The Steadfast Love of the Lord

The steadfast love of the Lord never ceases, his mercies never come to an end; they are new every morning; great is your faithfulness.

Steadfastness in Christ

Wherefore, you must press forward with a steadfastness in Christ, having a perfect brightness of hope, and a love of God and of all men. Wherefore, if you shall press forward, feasting upon the word of Christ, and endure to the end, behold thus says the Father, "Ye shall have eternal life."

II Nephi 13:29-30.

MEDITATION: Prayer

"For the sake of the gospel,"
O God, that is my plea.
For the sake of the gospel help me to lay aside all pettiness and meanness of spirit.
For the sake of the gospel let me find ways to overcome conflict and divisions.
Yet for the sake of the gospel may I not substitute what is not gospel for the gospel or compromise the gospel out of fear or betray the gospel out of self-interest.
For the sake of the gospel help me to stand fast for the gospel.
For the sake of the gospel help me to be faithful to the gospel.
And, finally, O God, for the sake of the gospel enable me above all, to distinguish what is gospel from what is not the gospel.
For the sake of the gospel enable me to discern the line I must never cross.
For the sake of the gospel enable me to know when to yield and when to stand fast.
Through Jesus Christ, your gospel. Amen.

E. Glenn Hinsen, "Reconciliation and Resistance," *Weavings* (November/December 2000).

With a Steadfast Faith

With a steadfast faith together let us walk
As we seek the Father's mind;
In our daily task and in his word revealed
His eternal purpose find.

With a steadfast faith together let us walk
That each one on earth may know
The abundant life, the way his Son has taught,
And in Christ-like stature grow.

With a steadfast faith together let us walk
Serving with a common heart,
Sharing gratefully the Spirit's constant care
And to all his love impart.

L. Wayne Updike. *Hymns of the Saints,* # 479.

What does it mean to you to be steadfast in the faith? How do you deal with temptations to forget it? What in your experience helps you to hold fast perhaps when you would rather not?

PRAYER: My God, I trust you and your guiding presence in my life. Help me to hear your voice clearly and have strength to follow it, I pray. Amen.

FRIDAY, THE THIRD WEEK OF LENT: FORGIVE US OUR TRESPASSES

SCRIPTURE: **John 20:19-23 Forgiveness Through the Holy Spirit**
"Receive the Holy Spirit"
Matthew 18:21-22 How Often Should I Forgive?
Then Peter came and said to him, "Lord, if another member of the church sins against me, how often should I forgive? As many as seven times?" Jesus said to him, "Not seven times, but I tell you, seventy-seven times."

MEDITATION: The Gift of Forgiveness

"Receive the Holy Spirit. If you forgive the sins of any, they are forgiven them; if you retain the sins of any, they are retained."

(John 20:22-23)

This was the Easter greeting of Jesus to his gathered and frightened disciples on the day of the resurrection. He came, bringing them the gift of forgiveness.

We must not underestimate the gift. The pagan world knew nothing of forgiveness – only fate. The good news of the Old Testament was that God forgave, and that through faith in new beginnings, God acted in the brokenness of his people. In the New Testament, Jesus himself forgave and in doing so bore the criticism and the accusation of blasphemy that brought him to his death.

Yet, his first words to his disciples is to share with them the incredible good news that the Spirit of God's own forgiving love dwells within us, and that the power to be forgiven and to forgive has been entrusted to us.

Forgiveness awaits us in the heart and hands of the Risen Jesus, in the hearts and hands of our fellow Christians. Jesus' words to the disciples invite us to bring the burden of our sinfulness, our brokenness, our need for forgiveness to another. "Confess you sins to one another" (James 5:16). . . .It can be a deepening of the healing to make a "confession," that is, to share with another one's need for healing and forgiveness.

Jacqueline Syrup Bergan and S. Marie Schwan,
Forgiveness: A Guide for Prayer (Saint Mary's Press, 1985), 139.

Forgiveness — The Way To Freedom

Community is not possible without the willingness to forgive one another "seventy-seven times." Forgiveness is the cement of community life. Forgiveness holds us together through good time and bad times, and it allows us to grow in mutual love. . . .

To forgive another person from the heart is an act of liberation. We set that person free from the negative bonds that exist between us. We say, "I no longer hold your offense against you." But there is more. We also free ourselves from the burden of being the "offended one." As long as we do not forgive those who have wounded us, we carry them with us or, worse, pull them as a heavy load. The great temptation is to cling in anger to our enemies and then define ourselves as being offended and wounded by them. Forgiveness, therefore, liberates not only the other but also ourselves. It is the way to the freedom of the children of God.

From Henri Nouwen, *Bread for the Journey*

Forgiveness: Remembering Without Rancor

Forgiving does not require us to forget but to remember without rancor. To remember well is to hold both the victim and the victimizer in God's grace, with prayer for every form of healing and blessing for both. God's project in the world is to redeem all, heal all, bless all. When the gift of forgiveness has freed us from our desire to condemn and punish the guilty one, we need not assume that all evidence of our wound will be gone. The risen Christ still bore on his body the marks of his crucifixion. But his scars were transfigured into signs of his victory over sin and death and have become for us a promise of participation in Jesus' victory as well

Companions in Christ: The Way of Forgiveness
(Upper Room Books, 2002) 98

Confess

The word "confess" has a twofold thrust: we confess our sins and we confess our faith. The hymn "Beneath the Cross of Jesus" expresses both of these meanings:

And from my stricken heart with tears
Two wonders I confess –
The wonders of redeeming love,
And my unworthiness.

Standing in the presence of our Lord we see our sin and confess our unworthiness. It is the experience Moses had as recorded in Section 22:7 of the Doctrine and Covenants: "Now, for this cause, I know that man is nothing, which thing I never had supposed; but now mine eyes have beheld God." That experience leads to the second use of the word "confess." - I vow my allegiance to the "wonders of redeeming love." Our Christian experience is incomplete without both of these. As Marjorie Suchocki has expressed it, "The tragedy of a church that confesses only its faith and not its sin, is that if it cannot confess its corporate sin, how can it truly confess faith?" "Without the church's confession of sin," she continues, "God's most powerful force for social renewal is left immobilized, locked away in a spiral of individualism that addresses only individual problems and ignores the dimensions of all personal sins. . . . We thus confess the mote and ignore the log."

Velma Ruch

What has been your experience with forgiving and receiving forgiveness? What do you find most difficult? In memory recall one or two experiences in which forgiveness was an issue?

PRAYER:

Father, when in love to thee Low we bow the adoring knee.
When repentant to the skies Scarcely do we lift our eyes.
Then, O hear us as we plead For thy help in time of need;
On thy mercy we rely; Hear, forgive us when we cry.

We repent the times we've stood For the things of lesser good,
And for stewardship of time We have spent unlinked with thine.
In the midst of sin and strife, Teach us how to live a life
Marked by graces of new birth, Worthy of thy saints on earth.

Father, while we look to thee, Lowly on the bended knee,
And in penitence we turn, For thy pardon now we yearn.
Reconcile us by thy love; Lift our souls to things above;
As we humbly now draw nigh, Hear, forgive us when we cry. Amen

Robert Grant, *Hymns of the Saints,* # 116.

SATURDAY, THE THIRD WEEK OF LENT: SACRAMENTAL LIFE

SCRIPTURE: **Doctrine and Covenants 85:3b The Light Which Is in All Things**

The light which is in all things; which giveth life to all things; which is the law by which all things are governed, even the power of God who sitteth upon his throne, who is in the bosom of eternity, who is in the midst of things.

Doctrine and Covenants 28:9a All Things Unto Me Are Spiritual

Verily I say unto you, that all things unto me are spiritual, and not at any time have I given unto you a law which was temporal.

Doctrine and Covenants 158:11c Look Especially to the Sacraments

Look especially to the sacraments to enrich the spiritual life of the body. Seek for greater understanding of my purposes in these sacred rites and prepare to receive a renewed confirmation of the presence of my Spirit in your experiences of worship.

MEDITATION: A Spiritual Universe

The wonder of this spiritual universe of which we are a part is that God has chosen to reveal himself through matter, through creation. It found its highest expression through the "Word that became flesh." Thus it is that we call the created world sacramental and we, as a part of that world, have sacramental potential as we become revealers of the presence of the Divine.

A sacramental universe means that we worship a God who is revealed in the local as well as the universal. This makes every place a potential bearer of the Holy. Experiencing God in a local setting makes it more possible for us to discover the Holy in other places. Time as well as space partakes of more than the now. It is now and always. Each moment, if we are aware, carries with it news of the Eternal.

A sacramental universe calls us to practice "everyday sacredness." It is what has been referred to increasingly as "practicing the presence." This means that our spiritual lives cannot be focused merely on Sunday morning or Wednesday evening, but must be part of every aspect of our lives, every moment of every day. That is the effort of a lifetime and needs to be supported and sustained by the church. It means that we have to look at the world with "sacred eyes." Such a vision allows us to penetrate to the essence of all things, to see into the divinity that gives them life and beauty. Then we know, too, something of our own essence, what it is that gives life meaning and purpose.

Velma Ruch, *The Transforming Power of Prayer*, Vol. 1 (Herald House, 1999) 118.

Sacramental Life

What if we were to approach every day as if we were entering a service of one of the church sacraments? Imagine the reverence of such days, the expectation of experiencing God's Spirit, the attentiveness to God's movement and the sacredness of those moments.

What if we were to approach every day the way many people do when they are experiencing a potentially terminal illness? Imagine the change of priorities, the new meanings and perspectives on life and relationships, the change of pace, and the connection with things previously unnoticed. These reflections perhaps give us a glimpse into living sacramentally.

It is in context of this extended view of sacrament that I am feeling my life challenged and reawakened. Certainly the formal sacraments are a major part of that journey as focal points of symbol and metaphor illuminating my everyday experience..... the way these experiences have touched my very being has reminded me that these sacred rites are doors to a sacramental life – where the Divine is welcomed with open arms and "and the spiritual life of the body is enriched." . . . .

"Abide in me as I abide in you" (John 15:4). . . .The abiding immediacy of God allows each of us to "abide in" and experience God's presence in our everyday walk of life. What a profound gift of God's grace! What an amazing sense of the sacramentality of life! In this view of life God is available to all – including the downtrodden, marginalized people of the world.

David M. Heinze, "The Sacramental Life,"
Herald (February, 2005) 16, 17.

Holy Ground

Holy Ground is the stable place of clarity and confidence in a turbulent human landscape of shifting values, crumbling hopes, frayed trusts, uncertain commitment. Holy Ground is the place of life-giving rootedness in something larger than our own lives, something deep enough and enduring enough to keep us anchored and oriented in the storm. Holy ground is the place at once attractive and fearsome, where God speaks and we listen, the place of empowerment, transformation and sending forth to live victoriously in a world too often disfigured by the defeat of justice, peace, and human dignity, the place where the gracious rule of God is known and the new creation becomes visible, the place where faith can move mountains.

John Mogabgab, *The Guide to Spiritual Discernment*
(Upper Room Books, 1996), 30.

Do This in Remembrance of Me

You have already been told to look to the sacraments to enrich the spiritual life of the body. It is not the form of the sacrament that dispenses grace, but it is the divine presence that gives life. Be respectful of tradition and sensitive to one another, but do not be unduly bound by interpretations and procedures that no longer fit the needs of a worldwide church.

Doctrine and Covenants, Section 162:2d

The inspired counsel received at the 2004 World Conference (D. and C. 162:2d) spoke deeply to my spirit in many ways. I found the quoted paragraph particularly encouraging. I have long felt that we have not been responding as fully as we should to the spiritual power available to us in the sacraments. We have consequently deprived ourselves of great blessings and opportunities to offer profound ministry to people in great need of the assurance of faith.

I am particularly concerned about our experiences with the Lord's Supper. This is the sacramental rite we all participate in on a regular basis. It is one of the two sacred ceremonies that nearly all Christians acknowledge to be sacramental (the other being baptism).. . .

[W}hen we understand this great gift in accordance with the riches of scripture and Christian tradition, we see how awesome and wonderful Communion as a church community really is, for Christ himself is present there!

Don H. Compier, "He Is Present at the Table,"
Herald, February, 2005, 20.

What experience have you had in attempting to live the sacramental life? What sacraments of the church have you experienced? Think of one of special significance to you.

PRAYER: God, who created us,
You offer us new life through your Son
and through the gift of your sacraments.
While I see new life all around me,
I don't always recognize the new life you offer.
Help me to grow this Lent in an awareness
of the gifts you place in my life
and in a greater appreciation for your care.
Give me the courage to ask for help. Amen
(From the Benedictine Sisters of Mt. Orab).

THE FOURTH WEEK OF LENT
THEME: THE PEOPLE WHO SAT IN DARKNESS HAVE SEEN A GREAT LIGHT

"The Lenten season too has its harbinger of spring, its brief taste of Easter during the fourth week. This day, known as *Laetare* or "Rejoice Sunday" (named for the first word of the traditional introit from Isaiah "Rejoice, O Jerusalem"), is celebrated with rose-colored vestments and a slight lightening of the solemn Lenten mood.....Many of the readings for *Laetare* Sunday capture the anticipatory mood by playing with the theme of light emerging from darkness. Mirroring the natural processes of the earth that is emerging from winter's limited daylight into the longer sunlit days of spring, the liturgical celebration plays with the light and darkness theme in a variety of ways."

Wendy M. Wright, *The Rising*
(Upper Room Books, 1994) 57-58.

SUNDAY, THE FOURTH WEEK OF LENT: THE RHYTHM OF LIGHT AND DARKNESS

SCRIPTURE: **Genesis 1:1-5 Let There Be Light**
Then God said, "Let there be light"; and there was light. And God separated the light from the darkness. God called the light Day and the, darkness he called Night.

John 1:1-14 And the Word Became Flesh
The light shines in the darkness and the darkness did not overcome it

Book of Mormon 3 Nephi 4:44-48 "I Will Be Your Light."
"I am the light and the life of the world. I am Alpha and Omega, the beginning and the end".

MEDITATION: Let There Be Light

At the beginning of time, God said, "Let there be light" and separated the light from the darkness. The light he called day and the darkness night. We tend to think of light as good and darkness bad but it is not always so. God established a rhythm in our lives in which dark and light were inextricably related. It is connected to the seasons, to our aging, to the death and resurrection that is so much a part of our lives. But darkness certainly can be bad and it raises the whole question of evil and suffering and how a God of light and love can allow that to be. We learned more about that and about God when at a certain point in time the Word became flesh and dwelt among us. Jesus said, "I am the light and the life of the world. I am Alpha and Omega, the beginning and the end (3 Nephi 4:48) and "I will also be your light in the wilderness" (Nephi 5:77) John testifying about Jesus wrote, "What has come into being in him was life, and the life was the light of all people. The light shines in the darkness, and the darkness did not overcome it" (John 1: 4-5). John added, "To all who received him, who believed on his name, he gave power to become the children of God" (John 1:10) and that most foundational of all scriptures in the New Testament, "For God so loved the world that he gave his only begotten Son that whoso believeth on him should not perish but have everlasting life" (John 3:16). That is where we come in. It is only as we seek the light of the world that we shall find wholeness and healing. In that journey we will know both darkness and light, but our call is that we, too, like Christ shall become light for the world. It is a call not only to companionship with Christ but to assume our responsibility as partners in the great redemptive work of Christ.

Velma Ruch

The Inner Light

The Inner Light, the Inward Christ, is no mere doctrine, belonging peculiarly to a small religious fellowship, to be accepted or rejected as a mere belief. It is the Living Center of reference for all Christian souls and Christian groups - yes, and of non-Christian groups as well – who seriously mean to dwell in the secret place of the Most High. He is the center and source of action, not the end-point of thought. He is the locus of commitment, not a problem for debate. Practice comes first in religion, not theory or dogma. And Christian practice is not exhausted in outward deeds. These are the fruits, not the roots.

Thomas R. Kelly, *A Testament of Devotion*
(Harper and Bros., 1941), 34-35.

Light Invisible and Visible

T. S. Eliot's pageant, *The Rock*, ends with a paean to both the visible light – our creation ennobled by the light of sun, moon, and stars – and the Invisible Light, the Light of the Divine which we speak of as Holy Spirit or Endowment:

O Light Invisible, we praise Thee!
Too bright for mortal vision.
O Greater Light, we praise Thee for the less;
The eastern light our spires touch at morning,
The light that slants upon our western doors at evening.
The twilight over stagnant pools at batflight,
Moon light and star light, owl and moth light,
Glow-worm glowlight on a grassblade.
O Light Invisible, we worship Thee!
We thank Thee for the lights that we have kindled,
The light of altar and of sanctuary;
Small lights of those who meditate at midnight
And lights directed through the coloured panes of windows
And light reflected from polished stone,
And gilded, carven wood, the coloured fresco.
Our gaze is submarine; our eyes look upward
And see the light but see not whence it comes.
O Light Invisible, we glorify Thee!

* * *

We thank Thee who hast moved us to building, to finding,
to forming at the ends of our fingers and beams of our eyes.
And when we have built an altar to the Invisible Light,

we may set thereon the little lights for which our bodily
vision is made.
And we thank Thee that darkness reminds us of light.
O Light Invisible, we give Thee thanks for Thy great glory

PRAYER: O Lord my God, who sent Jesus the light of the world, enlighten and protect me. Show me when and how to bask in your abundant and beautiful grace. Help me know when and how to seek your face. Give me confidence to look for your goodness as long as I live. Through Jesus Christ our Lord, Amen.

Glandion Carney

MONDAY, THE FOURTH WEEK OF LENT: IN A DARK TIME THE EYE BEGINS TO SEE

SCRIPTURE: **Matthew 4:16 Darkness and Light**

The people who sat in darkness have seen a great light, and for those who sat in the region and shadow of death light had dawned.

Psalm 40:1-3 He Set My Feet Upon a Rock

I waited patiently for the Lord; he inclined to me and heard my cry. He drew me up from the desolate pit, out of the miry bog, and set my feet upon a rock, making my steps secure.

MEDITATION: Moving Toward the Light

Theodore Roethke begins his poem "In a Dark Time" with the words, "In a dark time the eye begins to see." It is in such a dark time, if we do not allow ourselves to be numbed by the experience, that we feel most intensely and are most ready for the light of the Divine. That light can revolutionize our vision, penetrate our hurt with healing warmth, and give us courage.....

Cleo Hanthorne Moon writes of such an experience in her poem "Direction":

I am so blind, Lord,
I cannot see the clearing
I only feel my way
By the restraining thorn.
I do not dare trust my foot's direction,
Feeling for paths
In unsure error worn.
Speak to my mind,
Direct my true alignment,
Light my dim eyes,
My certainty increase.
Out of the maze of self and narrow vision,
Lead me to mount the high lookout of peace.

Cleo Hanthorne Moon, *Poetic Voices of the Restoration,* 17.

Velma Ruch, *Summoned to Pilgrimage*, 97-98

A Holy Dark

The week before Easter I began to sink into an inscrutable inner darkness unlike any I had ever experienced.. . . .

I sat on my bed, cradled my journal in my lap, and poured out my thoughts and feelings.

Palm Sunday. I feel as if a candle has blown out inside me. Earlier today I read a passage from New Seeds of Contemplation in which Merton said that if the person who has come upon the spiritual dark night is carried away with impatience, "he will run away from the darkness, and do the best he can to dope himself with the first light that comes along." That's my temptation. This idea of remaining in the darkness is foreign to me. I'm a light-seeking creature and an impatient one at that. But could it be that seeking light, real light, not the artificial stuff, comes only by dwelling for a time in the dark? (Dear Lord, I don't think I can stand one more paradox!)

The darkness gets excruciating. In fact, the other word that sums up my darkness is tension. In this dark cave of my own being, I'm brought into sharper contact with my pain. At night shadows that I can't see in daylight play on the wall. I see my wounds, my conflicts, my incompleteness, and my longing in heightened outlines on the walls of my soul.

I'd like to be rid of this darkness. To unwrap the cocoon. Get busy. Do something to take my mind off my "suffering," latch onto some easy neon answer that will camouflage the shadows. But I have the sense lurking inside that there's a mystery unfolding in the darkness that can't come any other way.

Could it be that this is a holy dark?

I closed my journal, then wrapped my arms around my knees and let the tears flow quietly from my eyes. They ran in tiny rivulets down my bare legs. I watched them, sensing that they were the birth waters in which I would become new.

Sue Monk Kidd, *When the Heart Waits* (Harper San Francisco, 1990)
Published in *Alive Now* (January/February, 1994) 52-53.

Then your light will break forth like the dawn
and your healing will quickly appear;
then your righteousness will go before you
and the glory of the lord will be your rear guard.
Then you will call, and the Lord will answer;
you will cry for help, and he will say, "Here am I."

Isaiah 58:8-9 NIV

PRAYER: Inspiration Through Newman's Prayer Hymn

The church asked me (Velma) for a period of time to minister in Norway (1986-88). It was not an easy place to minister with very few members, many of them among the bruised and brokenhearted themselves. It was difficult in the circumstances we faced to form a truly vibrant community, though the power of the Spirit was with us many times in rich measure. One day, however, as I was walking the snowy streets of Oslo feeling discouraged and alone, I asked myself the question, Why am I here? What am I called to do in this time and place? What good, if any, am I doing here? Is there any hope for the church in Norway? As I walked along I suddenly discovered I was humming Newman's great hymn, "Lead Kindly Light." In my mind I concentrated on the words:

Lead, kindly Light, amid the encircling gloom,
Lead thou me on.
The night is dark, and I am far from home,
Lead thou me on.

That became my prayer. I knew it had been Newman's prayer when he was in the midst of a serious illness that threatened his life. He wanted to serve the church but was not sure how. He was mentally and spiritually adrift. But as he wrote his feelings in the hymn that has blessed so many, his trust in the living God came to the fore and he wrote,

So long thy power hath blessed me, sure it still
Will lead me on,
O'er moor and fen, o'er crag and torrent, till
The night is gone;

> our civilization. I know which of these alternatives I must choose; but I cannot make this choice in security.

He set his face steadfastly toward his Jerusalem and before long was imprisoned. He ministered to the prisoners there for two yeas before he was executed on April 9, 1945. In Letters from Prison he wrote:

> I believe that God both can and will bring forth good out of evil. For that purpose he needs us who make the best use of everything. I believe God will bring us all the power we need to resist in times of stress.

We do not know what the future holds in store for us or what commitments will be demanded. In the meantime, by surrendering our lives to Christ we will be ready to give what is required.

PRAYER:

All to Jesus I surrender; All to him I freely give.
I will ever love and trust him In his presence daily life.

All to Jesus I surrender; Make me, Savior, wholly thine.
Let me feel the Holy Spirit Truly know that thou art mine.

All to Jesus I surrender; Lord, I give myself to thee.
Fill me with thy love and power; Let thy blessings fall on me.

Judson w. Van de Venter, *Hymns of the Saints,* # 430.

And with the morn those angel faces smile
Which I have loved long since, and lost awhile.

That was exactly what happened to me that day. All at once all my troubles dropped from me. I was enfolded in peace and love and made to know that the people were in God's hands. His love for them was greater than my love could possibly be. My responsibility was to do the best I could in the circumstances in which I found myself. A burden was lifted and I was free to minister.

Velma Ruch

In the Region and Shadow of Death

We hear the affirmation that occurs both in the Old and New Testaments: "The people who sat in darkness have seen a great light, and for those who sat in the region and shadow of death light has dawned." (Isa. 9:2; Mt. 4:16) Have we not all at some time sat in the region and shadow of death? This is not an experience one avoids by being a Christian. Life is full of devastation, of suffering and darkness. Such darkness can be absolutely devastating to us, but if we are rooted and grounded in love our grief may be no less and our suffering may still be intense, but we know that we do not go through the water and fire alone. It was of this Isaiah reminded us so long ago:

> *But now thus says the Lord, he who created you, O Jacob, he who formed you, O Israel; do not fear for I have redeemed you, I have called you by name, you are mine. When you pass through the waters, I will be with you and through the rivers they shall not overwhelm you; when you walk through fire you shall notbe burned, and the flame shall not consume you. For I am the Lord your God, the Holy One of Israel.*
>
> (Isaiah 43:17).

How has the light of the world come to you in difficult times? Do you have the sense that you are never alone, that whatever the circumstances that God is walking with you? Has it been possible for you, as Thomas Kelley expressed it, "to rise radiant in the sacrament of pain" ?

PRAYER: O God, you yourself through Christ have known what it is to walk through water and fire in its many manifestation. You have suffered with us and for us and your tears are shed for our sorrows. Our gratitude to you is inexpressible for this great gift. Reason does not tell us it is so, but our heart speaks in overflowing love to you. We trust in you. Amen.

TUESDAY, THE FOURTH WEEK OF LENT: THE LIGHT WHICH NOW SHINES

SCRIPTURE: **Doctrine and Covenants 85:3 a-b The Light Which Is In All Things**

And the light which now shineth, which giveth you light, is through him, who enlighteneth your eyes, who is the same light that quickeneth your understandings; which light proceedeth forth from the presence of God, to fill the immensity of space.

MEDITATION: The Light That Fills the Immensity of Space

God's great command as described in Genesis, "Let there be light," came before any other aspect of creation – four days before the creation of the sun, the moon, and the stars. It was the Word, the Logos, that was to penetrate all of creation, a light that proceeds from the Divine "to fill the immensity of space." It not only enlightens the eyes but illuminates our understanding and our very beings. Christ, the Light of the world, is indeed in the sunshine as in all created things, but is also the very light that is God.

Velma Ruch , *The Signature of God*, 186.

The Experience of Saint Augustine

In Augustine's nineteen-year-long search for an understanding of the Divine, his most important turning point came when he arrived at the concept of spirit, something that was real but not corporeal, perceptible, but not with the outer senses. In Book 7 of *Confessions* he attempts to describe this illumination that is not of the sun or of any material substance:

> Being thus admonished to return to myself, under your leadership I entered into my inmost being. This I could do, for you became my helper. I entered there and by my soul's eye, such as it was, I saw above the same eye of my soul, above my mind, an unchangeable light. It was not this common light, plain to all flesh, nor a greater light, as it were of the same kind, as though that light would shine many, many times more bright, and by its power fill the whole universe. Not such was that light, but different, far different from all other lights. Nor was it above my mind, as oil is above water, or sky above earth. It was above my mind because it made me, and I was beneath it, because I was made by it. He who knows the truth, knows that light, and he who knows it knows eternity. Love knows it, O eternal truth, and true love, and beloved eternity! You are my God and I sigh for you day and night.

The Confessions of Saint Augustine, John K. Ryan, trans.
(Image Doubleday, 1960) 170.
Velma Ruch, *Summoned to Pilgrimage*, 105.

The Light Became Flesh

The light is shining, it is a light that defies our ability to capture and define. The light has a voice that speaks life to us; the light has hands that hold and heal us. The light has a name – Jesus, the son of Mary, the Son of God.

The light became flesh. The light conquers darkness, and turns death into life. In situations as ordinary as a catering problem at a wedding or as deeply troubling as a death in the family, this light beams a transforming power. When the light is present in us, everything is changed. When the light is present in us, we are changed. We have eternal life. We are restored to the glory that our Creator God intended.

The Spiritual Formation Bible, Introduction to the Gospel of John.

Saints Are Not Born To It

Saints are not born to it
Except most rarely
Nor by default
Do they
Come to God
Having no other choice
But rather
Like sunflowers
Growing outside my door,
Do they grow and turn
Following the course
Of God
With upturned faces
Growing each day
Taller, stronger
More resistant
To the wind
Of the world,
And even in the times
Without sun,
They wait
Turned toward dawn,
Knowing the promise of light.
In their holy simplicity
The saints of God
Remember what I forget
Too easily -
That having found the sun,
The source of life
Just once,
All other light,
However strong
Is not enough.

Anne Squire Buresh

PRAYER: Light of Life, we thank you for your great glory and praise you for the beauty of your countenance as it smiles upon us. You give us light and breath and joy. We can truly exclaim with Paul, "Not I, but God in me." For this, we bow in adoration before you. Amen.

WEDNESDAY, THE FOURTH WEEK OF LENT: THE LORD IS MY LIGHT AND MY SALVATION

SCRIPTURE: **Psalm 27 Whom Shall I Fear?**
The Lord is my light and my salvation; whom shall I fear? The Lord is the stronghold of my life; of whom shall I be afraid?

John 8:12 Jesus, the Light of the World
And Jesus spoke to them, saying, "I am the light of the world. Whoever follows me will never walk in darkness but will have the light of life.

Isaiah 60:1-3 Arise, Shine, for Your Light Has Come
Arise, shine; for your light has come, and the glory of the Lord has risen upon you.

MEDITATION: Preparing for the Light

An important way of preparing ourselves for the presence of the Spirit is to let down the barriers that keep the Light out. There are ever so many ways we can do that. One is by taking a purely rationalistic approach that holds as valid only those experiences that can be reasonably explained and analyzed. God has to be found at the end of a syllogism or not at all. Another is by rejection because of our fear of the cost involved, the surrender of our wills. Such surrender is exceedingly difficult. We do not want a righteousness that can come to us only from God. We want to keep ourselves under our own control, make our own plans. Another way is by deliberately numbing our responses to overcome the pain of the longing. We can endure it so long and then we strive to change our anxiety into a prosperous sense of normalcy. We can give ourselves to the ritual of church-going, committee meetings, church drives, annual reports, etc. and become accustomed through great activity to live in a cooled and slowed-down faith. Once we overcome the barriers that have kept the Light out we wonder why it took us so long and why we were content with the meager when we could have the abundant.

Velma Ruch *Summoned to Pilgrimage, 110.*

The Golden Rule in Theology

Truth must be searched for with all the resources at our command. If we have been fortunate enough to be touched by the light of sacred knowledge, that "light which we have gained," John Milton reminds us, "was given us, not to be ever staring at but by it to discover onward things more remote from our knowledge. . . . To be still searching what we know not by what we know," he continues, "still closing up truth to truth as we find it. . . this is the golden rule in theology as well as in arithmetic, and makes up the best harmony in a church; not the forced and outward union of cold and neutral and inwardly divided minds."

"Areopagitica"

Prayer: *The Lord is my shepherd, I shall not want...*
He maketh me to lie down in green pastures;
He leadeth me beside the still waters.
He restoreth my soul;

He leadeth me in the paths of righteousness for his name's sake.
Yea, though I walk through the valley of the shadow of death,
I will fear no evil, for thou art with me,
Thy rod and thy staff they comfort me.
Thou preparest a table before me in the presence of mine enemies;
Thou anointest my head with oil, my cup runneth over.
Surely goodness and mercy shall follow me all the days of my life;
And I will dwell in the house of the Lord forever. Amen.

THURSDAY, THE FOURTH WEEK OF LENT: LET YOUR LIGHT SHINE

SCRIPTURE: **Ephesians 5:8-14 Live as Children of Light**

For once you were in darkness, but now in the Lord you are light. Live as children of light – for the fruit of the light is found in all that is good and right and true.

Matthew 5:14-16 You Are the Light of the World

"You are the light of the world. A city built on a hill cannot be hid. No one after lighting a lamp puts it under the bushel basket, but on the lamp stand and it gives light to all the house. In the same way, let your light shine before others, so that they may see your good works and give glory to your father in heaven."

MEDITATION: A Keeper of the Lantern

Many around us are journeying on roads that may be very dark. To them we can be a light. Bess Streeter Aldrich once wrote a book called A Lantern in Her Hand. In it she wrote:

Because the road was steep and long
And through a dark and lonely land,
God set upon my lips a song
And put a lantern in my hand.

It is a tremendous responsibility to be a keeper of the lantern. We never know when we shall hear a cry from the dark, when we may be the only person able to help in that place at that time. These cries often come to us without warning, cries from the lonely, the confused, the depressed. We know that our little light will not banish the dark, but when it is joined by the Light of Christ we can expect miracles even in the most difficult of circumstances

Be a Light Here and Now

Anyone who has ever borne a light through the dark knows that it does not do away with the darkness – *but it shows a way through it* and that is something I have to bear in mind, as I bear the lamp of God's light in Christ forward into any dark place. And there are many such parts of our world today, in personal and in public affairs. Here and there, often without warning, comes an accident, a cry of bewilderment, a grave illness, a tangled business relationship, an experience of intense loneliness, or a dark family relationship made up of subtle behavior – and it is hard to find a clear, safe way ahead. It is at that moment when Christ's words come ringing clear: *"Let your light shine. . . and not to your own praise, but to the Glory of God, your Father!"* For it is God who makes this possible and supplies any light that is to be had in any dark circumstance; human effort, human wisdom is not enough. It is then that we need what he makes available in Christ – mediated through human friends, teachers, neighbors, "lights" he has set near to our lives here and now. . . .

Another thing is that a light is not a rowdy, pretentious thing, but a *wordless witness.* So any one of us can bear the light entrusted to us. We may not be clever enough theologically to argue the things of God that have bearing on our journey through the world – but if they are real in our experience, through the mercy and love of Christ, we can witness to them by our faithful living. It might well be a silent affair, as silent as holding a lantern high. We are all capable of that much in the life we live, in the place where we live, 'here and now.'. . .

And the call is: *"Let your light shine,"* – not somebody else's but some light real to you, a gift from the great Light of the World to you, experienced and tested, and rejoiced in by you! Florence Allshorn liked to speak of an RAF pilot who said to a Christian with whom he came into contact: "Don't try to help me or preach to me or tell me what I ought to think yet. Don't work for my salvation. Show me yours!" That's the simple secret, all anyone can do with a light: hold it high! It is one's witness that is unique, distinctive, unlike any other faith in this world – witness to Jesus Christ, above all, and to the glory of God! The very first Christians had no greater challenge, the greatest saints, the humblest sinners – it is still our privilege to do no more, no less, than keep our light high and burning.

Rita Snowden, *I Believe Here and Now* (Great Britain: Fount Paperbacks, 1981)
Excerpts 142-146.

Walk In The Light

Walk in the light; so shalt thou know, that fellowship of love
His Spirit only can bestow, Who reigns in light above.

Walk in the light, and thou shalt find Thy heart made truly his,
Who dwells in cloudless light enshrined, in whom no darkness is.

Walk in the light and thou shalt own Thy darkness passed away,
Because that light has on thee shone In which is perfect day.

Walk in the light, and thine shall be A path, though thorny, bright,
For God by grace shall dwell in thee, And God himself is light.

Bernard Barton, *Hymns of the Saints,* # 303.

PRAYER: God of Light and Salvation, you who are Light itself have called us, finite as we are, to be reflectors of that light. We are humbled to be so chosen, but we know that it is only through your power and love that we can so serve. Forgive us for the times that we forget and take pride in what we perceive as our own accomplishment or refuse to serve because we do not trust in your promised endowment. Help us to remember that you are always near and it is through that Presence we truly live. Amen.

FRIDAY, THE FOURTH WEEK OF LENT: LIVING IN THE PRESENCE

SCRIPTURE: **Book of Mormon Alma 17:68-70 Let All Your Doings Be unto God**
Book of Mormon, Moroni 7:52-53 Christian Identity

MEDITATION: God As Center of Our Whole Being

In the selected text from Alma 17, Alma takes up the issue of the daily sojourn of the Christian. This sojourn is sustained from the human side by a determination to live obediently day by day. "Learn in your youth," Alma says, "to keep the commandments of God." And yet the text does not envision the relationship between God and human beings as merely legal. In the very next line lies the key to the whole journey: "cry to God for all your support" (17:68). Inner power – a power not our own – is needed for obedient walking in the way of Christ. Only God can give what God asks of us; our asking for support in all things is an admission of our need of grace. Grace is a gift of God's own presence, and it is God's own presence that we need in us in order to keep the commandments. Doing is made possible by a state of being: our state of being can be blessed and healed only by Christ in us....The point of the Christian path is to let God become the center of the whole person. Our doing, our thinking, our feeling, our willing, and our dying – even our sleeping – are to be drawn into the orbit of worship...The way Alma enjoins for us is the way of prayer without ceasing.

Anthony Chvala-Smith, "Prayer in the Book of Mormon" in Ruch, *The Transforming Power of Prayer,* Vol. 1, 86-87.

Thirst for the Spirit

Religious experience has been defined as an encounter between God and the individual. If this is so, our entry to that experience is prayer. This immediately widens our conception of prayer as taking in all those times when we drink at the source of meaning. There may be no words spoken but we sense we have been in the Presence. Such an experience may come through the wind blowing in the pine trees or through another person. In a way this gives us a 'toe-hold" into divine presence, but God by giving makes us ask. Sensing presence through nature, through the beautiful, creates in us a thirst for something more. What we have experienced, as C. S. Lewis has observed, is "only the scent of a flower we have not found, the echo of a tune we have not heard, news from a country we have never visited." (The Weight of Glory, (William B. Eerdman, 1965, 5) A desire is built in us for a presence that can deal with us personally, that intersects with our spirits and to whom we can speak or simply rest in that enveloping love. What we long for is the Holy Spirit, that Jesus promised his disciples would soon be theirs. They had that experience on the day of Pentecost and were transformed into a prophetic people

Velma Ruch, *The Order of Evangelists' Training Resource,* 125.

Prayer and Formation of Christian Identity

(See Moroni, 7: 52-53)

I recently had an unusual experience with this passage. I occasionally take time during my workday for a prayer walk. Not long ago I left my desk one afternoon and went for such a walk. As I walked I prayed with words that the God of Mormon had taught me to pray, the words of Moroni 7:52-53. My prayer went something like this:

> God, I know my own weakness and fear. I am aware that my own hidden desires have the potential to corrupt the things I do, but you know my depths far better than I. But I believe that below the haze of my own sin, you have implanted in me through the gospel a desire to love with a love shaped by Christ alone. I ask that in the very depths of my soul the pure love of Christ will come to dwell more fully than ever. Grant me, Lord, first to love your Son, with depth and purity; and also grant that his own love will fill me more and more, until I am re-made into his image.

I have prayed variations of this prayer for years. This time, quite unexpectedly, I was flooded by the power of God. A love, deep and pure, surged up in my heart and grasped me deep within my soul. The sensation brought me to a halt; I just had to stop and stand there in awe for a few minutes. To describe what I experienced requires some metaphorical language: it was power, knowledge, and light, and it was all intensely personal. I understood that my prayer had been heard and my desire accepted, that God was in the process of answering this prayer step by step over the long journey of my life. As I stood there I felt a deep unity with my surroundings, but also with the saints who had gone before us in the Restoration movement. This all happened so quickly, but its effect will probably last the rest of my life.

Anthony Chvala-Smith, "Prayer in the Book of Mormon," in Velma Ruch, *The Transforming Power of Prayer* Vol. 1, 91-92.

PRAYER: O Holy One, great as you are you stoop to our weakness and ask for entrance to our hearts. When we respond, you bless us with daily grace and love. Our cup overflows in gratitude and we know the joy for which we were created. We thank you and with quickened step follow where you lead. Amen.

SATURDAY, THE FOURTH WEEK OF LENT: DIVERSITY OF GIFTS

SOME SCRIPTURES CONCERNING THE GIFTS:

1 Corinthians 12 Varieties of gifts but the Same Spiritt
1 Corinthians 13 And the Greatest of These Is Love
Romans 12 Grace and gifts That Differ
Ephesians 4 Gifts Given for Building Up the Body of Christ
Book of Mormon, Moroni 10:8-14 Deny Not the Gifts of God
Doctrine and Covenants 46:4-9 To Every Person Is Given a Gift

SOME AFFIRMATIONS REGARDING SPIRITUAL GIFTS:

1. All are called according to the gifts of God unto them. This is a basic belief of the church. It is saying that we all share responsibility for carrying on the work of the church.

2. God intends that the ministry of the church be accomplished through spiritual gifts. Human talents in and of themselves are not adequate for spiritual ministry. Paul declared: "Weak men we may be, but it is not as such we fight our battles. The weapons we wield are not merely human, but divinely potent to demolish strongholds." (2 Cor. 10: 3-4 NEB). Nothing less than the blessings and resources of the Divine will equip the church to meet the opportunities of this generation.

3. Discovering our call is a life-time process. We may know fairly early in our lives the general direction of the call, but we change, circumstances change and we may find that we are called to serve in different ways. Still there is likely to be a growing conviction of a central call.

4. A gift is a gift is a gift but is subject to discipline. We do not decide what gifts will be ours. It is a gift of the Spirit and subject to the Spirit's will. The discovery of our spiritual gifts is important because that leads us into the necessary discipline to enhance the gifts. One way to prepare and go about discovering is asking each day, "What does God want of me this day?" It helps set priorities. A help in answering this question is asking another, "Where is my deepest joy? In what activity do I find fulfillment? What are the special moments in my life?" That which brings us joy is an avenue to fulfillment that needs to be cultivated. One writer attempted to answer the question for all of us by saying, "My deepest joy comes in using the gifts God has given me to do the divine work in the world. It is doing something well and feeling fulfilled in doing it." A number of psychologists are coming to a similar conclusion. One started by trying to discover why it was that so many people lived miserable lives. That led him to look at the question from another point of view, "What is it that distinguishes people that live fulfilled lives?" He came to the conclusion that it involved satisfying work. It is a sense that we have a purpose for our

existence and we are alert to those occasions where we can give it our best expression.

5. There is more than one way to fulfill God's longing for us. Be aware of doors that open before you but be just as aware of those that close behind you. Sometimes we try to force open doors that would be better shut.

6. Whatever our call, a saying "yes" to the Lord is essential.

7. Needs and circumstances may alter how we express our commitment.

What in life gives you most joy? Are you aware of your own spiritual gifts? Do you grow in your expression of them? How? Name to yourself the gifts you believe are yours and think of at least one incident in which you felt blessed by the Spirit in the doing.

PRAYER: Loving God, we celebrate the diversity of talents and gifts you give to your people. Help us to see how we can use them for the common good. Amen.

THE FIFTH WEEK OF LENT
THEME: THE JOURNEY TO JERUSALEM

SUNDAY, THE FIFTH WEEK OF LENT: MINISTRY ALONG THE WAY

SCRIPTURE: **John 11:1-45 Mary, Martha, and Lazarus**

[Jesus] called with a loud voice, "Lazarus, come out!" The dead man came out, his hands and feet bound with strips of cloth, and his face wrapped in a cloth. Jesus said to them, "Unbind him and let him go."

MEDITATION: The Raising of Lazarus

The account of the raising of Lazarus is a wonder, marveled at by generations of Christians. It speaks of God's redemptive action in the midst of human life, of divine fulfillment of the ancient covenant in the person of Jesus. It proclaims Jesus as the Christ, the fount of eternal life.

Beyond this, the Johannine passage is an incredibly rich mine of images and ideas that can enliven its hearers. It contains the poignant account of Jesus' friendship with this family, the encounter with the weeping Mary with her distraught accusation – "If you had been here" – and Jesus' tearful response to her grief. Even more strikingly, it contains Martha's confession that Jesus is the Messiah, the Son of God. Except for the confession of Peter found in Matthew 16:16 (and the confession of Andrew to Peter in John 1:41), there is no other comparable statement of faith discovered in the gospels. For the early church, to confess Christ in this way was the mark of an apostle. Thus we have here a somewhat lost tradition, apparently current in the community from which the Gospel of John comes, of Martha as a first witness to Jesus as the resurrection, the one who brings new life.

The Lazarus passage, placed here strategically in the heart of Passiontide , speaks eloquently to me of hope and healing, especially as it is discovered in the communities of friendship in which we find ourselves. It is a Gospel that speaks of tears and compassion and the empathetic suffering we share with one another, a suffering which raises us beyond our own small sorrows and limited vision. It is a Gospel that proclaims the miracle of renewal that is discovered as we allow ourselves to know our interdependence. Our personal lifelessness, our private wounds are made whole as we tenderly touch and are touched by one another.

Wendy M. Wright, *The Rising* (The Upper Room, 1994), 71.

We Are All Lazarus

Timothy was a young priest whose wanderings, though intense, lasted only a short time. In his journal he recounted an experience that helped him understand this stage of his journey:

I was sitting quietly, and the story of Lazarus came to mind,
especially the moment when Jesus weeps, sighs, and calls Lazarus forth.
Then I felt myself enclosed in a tomb and I found myself removing layers,

> like blankets. At the first layer I asked for forgiveness for the self-idolatry ....Then came a deeper cover, I was reluctant to touch it, but I did. I pulled it off and a deep sigh came from my heart. Suddenly I was at a door – the same door that I had tried to open before. This time I gave it a hearty yank and it opened easily. Light fell in upon me immediately. An arm beckoned me to go through the door into this unknown world. I did, and I felt an embrace throughout my body. Then there was silence.
>
> I see now a new revelation from the story of Lazarus. We are all Lazarus bound up by the wraps of our own death and sin. In the aloneness of our hearts, we hear the voice cry, "Come out!" We peel the wrappings that bind us and stumble for the door and into the daylight of life and the loving arms of Jesus.

Timothy's new awareness prepared him to continue his journey...Then when we hear God call our name, we like Samuel, have the opportunity to answer, "Here I am."

Ron DelBene, *The Hunger of the Heart*
(Upper Room Books, 1992) 36-37.

From what in your own life do you need to be "unbound"? What are some ingrained habits in your life that are keeping you from truly responding to Christ's call to you?

How can you begin the process of eliminating these habits? Are you willing to commit yourself to that process and carry through?

PRAYER: Loving God, in deep humility I come before you recognizing how often I have failed in rising to the person you have called and gifted me to be. Grant me new eyes to see myself as you see me and courage to make the changes in my life that are necessary. I truly wish to be a worthy servant for you. Amen.

MONDAY, THE FIFTH WEEK OF LENT: WHO DO YOU SAY THAT I AM?

Jesus leaves Capernaum now to head north into the area of Caesarea Philippi and the Mount Hermon mountains. Here the River Jordan finds its source among mountain springs and streams. Our gospel companions invite us to join them in a quiet place near the villages of Caesarea Philippi. This is time of being with, of naming and knowing – a time for retreat before Jesus begins the long walk toward Jerusalem and all that awaits him there.

Wendy J. Miller, *Jesus, Our Spiritual Director*
(The Upper Room, 004), 141.

SCRIPTURE: Matthew 16:13-20 "You Are the Messiah, the Son of the Living God"

MEDITATION: Peter's Confession That Jesus Is the Messiah

In each of the Gospels {Peter's confession} is depicted as the first time anyone acknowledges the scope and extent of Jesus' life and thus becomes at least dimly aware of the nature of discipleship. Although each of the gospel narratives cast this confession in quite different ways, in each the coming passion is predicted. The path of discipleship is not simply a road to glory. It means walking in the way of the one who suffered and was rejected. . . . .

Throughout the centuries Jesus' pointed question to Peter, "Who do you say that I am?" has resonated through the Christian community. In one sense, the response, following Peter's lead, has been basically univocal, "You are the chosen one of God." You are the word that God wishes us to hear, the heart of God shown to us, the God-directed life acted out for us, the teacher God sends to instruct, the beloved child, the image that reflects our true selves back to us.

In another sense, our responses over the centuries have been multivocal. For each age has depicted Jesus differently, has allowed the good news to unfold in the unique peculiarities of time and place, has interpreted discipleship in light of present historical reality. This is, of course, the great challenge of Christianity, or any founded religion for that matter, to attempt with integrity to discern the original insights of the founder and to allow those insights to come alive in each succeeding age. Each language, each culture, each era refracts the gospel in somewhat variant ways. Just as each of the evangelists refracted the story of Jesus through the lens of the community for which he wrote, we come to the story with lenses of our own focused by the context of our lives. Yet we each must ask the same question, both for ourselves and in conversation with those with whom we worship and whom we would call brothers and sisters. "Who do you say that I am?"

Wendy M. Wright, *The Time Between*
(Upper Room Books, 1999), 108-110.

How Do We Know?

The question of <u>how</u> we know who Jesus is remains a crucial question for all of us. "Jesus' response to Simon's confession is warm and affirming: 'Blessed are you, Simon son of Jonah! For flesh and blood has not revealed this to you, but my Father in heaven" (Matt. 16:15-17). We along with Simon, are being invited by Jesus to learn about <u>how</u> we know. We can receive knowledge from rational, empirical human sources, but another source of knowing exists – revelation. Jesus reveals the heart of the new thing God is doing. No longer will a person's standing with God be built on keeping the law of Moses. Jesus is building the church – the household of God – on the sure foundation of believing he is the Messiah. We are transformed as we live into being children of God and sisters and brothers to one another. This is the great homecoming for which we all long."

Wendy J. Miller, *Jesus, Our Spiritual Director*
(Upper Room Books, 2004), 142.

The question, "How do I know?" is an important one. What are the major affirmations of your life? How did you come to them? If their origin in you has become dim, think back, retrieve and either reaffirm or give it a second look. If it is genuine, make it live again.

PRAYER: The Point of No Return
Never a pause, O Christ,
in your persistent questioning
"Who do you say that I am?"

You are the one who
loves me into endless life. . .

You kept on saying, live the little
bit of the Gospel you have grasped.
Proclaim my life. Light fire on the
earth . . . You, follow me. . .

Until one day I understand: you
were asking me to commit myself
to the point of no return.

Brother Roger, *A Life We Never Dared Hope For.*
Quoted in *Alive Now* (May/June 1993,) 65.

TUESDAY, THE FIFTH WEEK OF LENT: THE ROAD TO JERUSALEM

SCRIPTURE: **Matt. 16:21-27 "Deny Yourselves. Take Up Your Cross and Follow Me."**

MEDITATION: Setting Our Minds On God's Way

If the disciples are basking in the warmth of receiving spiritual insight into God's revelation about Jesus, quite suddenly their comfort level is shattered. Jesus informs them "he must go to Jerusalem and undergo great suffering at the hands of the elders and chief priest and scribes, and be killed, and on the third day be raised" (Matt 16:21). The words sound dark, impossible, unreal. Our gospel companions share with us their reaction of shock, denial, and disbelief. Their understanding of the Messiah does not include suffering and death.....

Peter walks Jesus away from the disciples a short distance and gives him a sharp rebuke: "God forbid it, Lord! This must never happen to you!" (Matt. 16:22). He calls on God to act in accordance with his own conception of the Messiah. Jesus turns his back on Peter and looks toward the rest of our disciple companions, his body language announcing the verbal rebuke he is about to give Peter: "Get behind me, Satan! You are a stumbling block to me; for you are setting your mind not on divine things but on human things" (v.23)....

The spiritual realm is not all benign. Jesus calls his disciples to discern what kind of spirit is at work within them as he explains to Peter, "You are setting your mind not on divine things but on human things."....

Whatever we worry about, strain after, become protective or violent about, and spend our life trying to save will, in the end, blind us to our real life – our soul and being. We will lose the very thing for which we have been concerned along with our true life and being; hence our need to pay attention to our hopes and desires. These things we offer to God; they become our sacrifice.

Wendy J. Miller, *Jesus, Our Spiritual Director*
(Upper Room Books, 2004), 142-145.

Commitment To Stay the Course

Setting one's face steadfastly means commitment all the way, regardless of the circumstances. It will never be easy, as it certainly was not for Jesus. He had moments, too, when he wondered about the cost, but hard as it was he never wavered. If we are to journey with Jesus, we, too, may wonder if we have the stamina to remain steadfast. But we remember, "No one having put his hand to the plough and looking back is fit for the kingdom of God."

The German theologian Dietrick Bonhoeffer is one who had the commitment to stay the course. He was at odds with Hitler's regime, but when it got worse in Germany he was safe in America. His conscience would not let him stay in safety. In a letter he wrote,

> I shall have no right to participate in the reconstruction of Christian life in Germany after the war if I do not share the trials of this time with my people...Christians in Germany will face the terrible alternative of either willing the defeat of their nation in order that Christian civilization may survive, or willing the victory of their nation and thereby destroying

WEDNESDAY, THE FIFTH WEEK OF LENT: THE TRANSFIGURATION

SCRIPTURE: **Luke 9:28-36 "This Is My Son, My Chosen; Listen to Him."**
From the cloud came a voice that said, "This is my Son, my Chosen; listen to him!" When the voice had spoken Jesus was found alone.

MEDITATION: On the Mountain

[In the Transfiguration] we have another of the great hinges in Jesus' life upon earth. We must remember that he was just about to set out to Jerusalem and to the cross. We have already looked at one great moment when he asked his disciples who they believed him to be, in order that he might discover if anyone had realized who he was. But there was one thing Jesus would never do – he would never take any step without the approval of God. In this scene that is what we see him seeking and receiving.

What happened on the Mount of Transfiguration we can never know, but we do know that something tremendous did happen. Jesus had gone there to seek the approval of God for the decisive step he was about to take. There Moses and Elijah appeared to him. Moses was the great law-giver of the people of Israel; Elijah was the greatest of the prophets. It was as if the princes of Israel's life and thought and religion told Jesus to go on.

Jesus could set out to Jerusalem now, certain that at least one little group of men knew who he was, certain that what he was doing was the consummation of all the life and thought and work of his nation, and certain that God approved of the step that he was taking.

There is a vivid sentence here. It says of the three apostles, "When they were fully awake they saw his glory." In life we miss so much because our minds are asleep....We would do well to pray "Lord, keep me always awake to you."

William Barclay, *The Gospel of Luke*
(The Westminster Press, 1975), 123-125.

How Good, Lord, To Be Here

Matthew 17: 4a *"Then Peter said to Jesus, "Lord, it is good for us to be here..."*

How good, Lord, to be here! Your glory fills the night;
Your face and garments, like the sun, Shine with unborrowed light.

How good, Lord, to be here! Your beauty to behold
Where Moses and Elijah stand, Your messengers of old.

Fulfiller of the past And hope of things to be,
We hail your body glorified And our redemption see.

Before we taste of death, We see your kingdom come;
We long to hold the vision bright And make this hill our home.

How good, Lord to be here! Yet we may not remain;
But since you bid us leave the mount, Come with us to the plain.

Joseph A. Robinson, *Lutheran Book of Worship*, 89.

Have you ever personally experienced a Mount of Transfiguration when you were lifted out of yourself and knew whose you were and where you were going.? Such experiences are turning points in our lives. They may not be as dramatic as Saul's experience on the road to Damascus or Isaiah's in the Temple but they are life changing nevertheless. In his poem "Vacillation" the Irish poet, W. B. Yeats wrote:

My fiftieth year had come and gone,
I sat, a solitary man,
In a crowded London shop,
An open book and empty cup
On the marble tabletop,
While on the shop and street I gazed
My body of a sudden blazed;
And twenty minutes more or less
It seemed, so great my happiness
That I was blessed and could bless.

These experiences may last only twenty minutes or less but they are what T. S. Eliot called "the still point." Such experiences are both in time and out of time, now and always. What do you remember of such experiences in your life?

PRAYER: Ever-Present God, you have blessed us so richly in a multitude of ways. We, too, have been blessed by standing on the mountain with you. We know with Peter what it means to be tempted to stay there, but the valley with its many needs looms before us. We know our mission is to the bruised and broken-hearted. May we be upheld as we walk with you down the mountain to bless as we were blessed. Amen.

THURSDAY, THE FIFTH WEEK OF LENT: AND WHEN THEY HAD COME DOWN FROM THE MOUNTAIN

SCRIPTURE: **Luke 9:37-43 The Healing of the Epileptic Boy**

On the next day, when they had come down from the mountain, a great crowd met him. Just then a man from the crowd shouted, "Teacher, I beg you to look at my son; he is my only child."

MEDITATION: Coming Down from the Mountain

No sooner had Jesus descended from the mountain top than the demands and disappointments of life were upon him. A man had come to the disciples seeking their help, for his only son was an epileptic.. . .It must have been a pitiful sight to see the lad convulsed; and the disciples were quite helpless to cure him. But when Jesus came he dealt with the situation with calm mastery and gave the boy back to his father cured.

Two things stand out:

(1) The moment on the mount was absolutely necessary, but it could not be prolonged beyond its own time. Peter, not really knowing what he was saying, would have liked to linger on the mountain top. He wished to build three tabernacles so that they might stay there in all the glory; but they had to descend again. Often there come to us moments that we would like to prolong indefinitely. But after the time on the mountain top we must come back to the battle and the routine of life; that time is meant to give us strength for life's everyday.. . .We cannot live forever in the moment on the mountain but we cannot live at all without it.

(2) In no incident is the sheer competence of Jesus so clearly shown. When he came down from the mountain the situation was out of hand. The whole impression is that of people running about not knowing what to do. The disciples were helplessly baffled; the boy's father was bitterly disappointed and upset. Into this scene of disorder came Jesus. He gripped the situation in a flash and in his mastery the disorder became a calm. So often we feel that life is out of control; that we have lost our grip on things. Only the Master of life can deal with life with the calm competence that brings everything under control.

William Barclay, *The Gospel of Luke*
(The Westminster Press, 1975), 125-127.

The Challenges of the Valley

Once God is discovered and we have felt the great joy of the words, "Whom thou soughtest, I am" or "I am the one who is speaking to you" or "Whom shall I send and who will go for us?" what then? First, like the disciples, we want to stay on the Mount of Transfiguration. After the great experience on the mountain , Peter said, "Master, it is good for us to be here. Let us make three dwellings, one for you, one for Moses, and for Elijah." The gospel writer's comment on that is interesting. He essentially said that Peter didn't know what he was talking about. And he didn't. The story ends, "On the next day when they had come down from the mountain..." We always come down from the mountain or as Browning expressed it to the C-Major of this life. It is in the valley, in the daily challenges of our living that the major work is done. The mountain gives us the inspiration and the courage, but it is in the valley that we learn what the experience meant, both the glory and the cost.

Velma Ruch

The C-Major of This Life

I personally have had experiences of coming down from the mountain after a supreme moment of choosing. I had been in Norway for a year and returned home for a few weeks. It happened that at that time I had to undergo emergency surgery. It was while I was still in the Independence Regional Health Center, three days after surgery, that I received a letter telling me of my call to the office of evangelist. Several experiences had prepared me for this moment, but the moment itself was one filled with the Holy Spirit and with joy. The next three weeks of recuperation from my surgery were a time in which I was lifted up in spirit and had a vision of what Christ had designed for the world. I read books about the ministry of the evangelist and was struck by statements such as, "The evangelist shoulders a thousand hurts so that others might be free." That sounded good to me. I wanted to be that kind of person.

Three weeks later I was ordained and within four days left for Norway. It took me just one day to realize that I was no longer on the mountaintop of spiritual exhilaration but that the desert loomed before me. The congregation to which I retuned was somehow different from the one I had left two months before. There were undercover tensions and animosities that expressed themselves in an incident that not only depressed but angered me. I could see all the work we had done going down the drain. I wondered what I was doing there at all and had the impulse to buy a ticket and come back home. I felt all alone with no one to turn to for help. Sometimes I think it may have been the Spirit that exaggerated these feelings in my mind, so that in my brokenness there would be room for learning.

I had read a great deal in the previous weeks about reconciliation. Now I was confronted with a desperate need for exactly that. I found that relieving the hurts of the world had a high price tag. I was alone. I had no one to turn to but God. The next three days, I believe I lived continually in the Spirit's presence, but it was by no means a mountaintop. It was the valley, it was desert, and it hurt. But in those three days I learned something about ministry and my role in it that I could never have learned on the heights.

Before Christ could truly lead me out of the desert, I had to overcome my own feelings of distress and loneliness and learn to look on our situation with love and concern for the people's welfare. Once that happened the Spirit taught me the way of resolution. I trusted that Spirit. In the resolution that followed we were all blessed and we loved one another with a new and special love.

Some days later I tried to record how I had felt during those days of desert learning. I wrote in my journal a statement that ended in these words:

> I was not and am not yet convinced how lasting the ministry I have tried to give will be. Some may breathe a sigh of relief when I leave. That does not matter. I have learned lessons about ministry on this rather lonely frontier with God, the people, and me. The lessons are not over and I must be prepared to continue to learn. I think I have come to understand the Christ better in these days than before and I wish to be able to reveal that understanding in reconciling ministry. This is

> my evening prayer on December 9, 1987. I do not know what further understandings lie ahead but I wish to have the courage to meet them in the way I should and to know what it is Christ would have of me in the days of my ministry.
>
> Velma Ruch, *Summoned to Pilgrimage*, 20-21.

What have been your experiences of coming down from the mountain? What did you learn from them?

PRAYER: How good, Lord, to be here! Yet we may not remain; But since you bid us leave the mount, Come with us to the plain. Amen

FRIDAY, THE FIFTH WEEK OF LENT: A SAMARITAN VILLAGE REFUSES TO RECEIVE JESUS

SCRIPTURE: **Luke 9:51-56 "Shall We Bid Fire to Come down from Heaven To Consume Them?"**

MEDITATION: Call Down Fire Out of Heaven

Call down fire out of heaven. It was the sort of thing young disciples might want to do. Scuttle the ship, block the pass, blow up the ungrateful so-and-sos! And therefore, says Mark, Jesus nicknamed James and John "Boanerges" – "sons of thunder." Or, if we follow Cranfill and others, sons of agitation and commotion.

There is an overweening confidence in the young, a kind of invincible optimism that they can remake the world in their generation....Jesus called youthful disciples, among others, and apparently he felt more attachment to young John – the teenager? – than to any of the others. But he also rebuked their eagerness to destroy their enemies, to have the kingdom in a cocked hat....It is not easy, is it, learning to be patient, to see the world with God's ancient eyes and then to wait a while longer? Or to be like Jesus on the cross, blessing one's enemies and crowning their worst efforts with forgiveness. Not easy at all. To the young it seems like failure. "Why didn't you smash them when you had the chance?" "What good is power if you don't use it?"

But there is mystery here, in the word of forgiveness ...Perhaps the mystery, or at least the point where mystery touches us most intimately. "Forgive them." Not blind rage, but "Forgive them." Not a fire out of heaven, but "Forgive them." Not a nuclear holocaust, but "Forgive them."....That is what we have to come to see when we are young, and what we have to do. We have to learn to love. And oh, it is so hard and takes so long for love really to become love and not mere rhetoric, for love to be caring – deep genuine caring – and not concern for one's own posture or image....That is the word from the cross – the word of patience and tolerance and knowing that in the long haul it is God who brings in the kingdom, not we ourselves.....

We don't make the world over by calling down fire from heaven; we do it by being there when people need us, when the crisis in life occurs and they are at a flashpoint of learning and seeing....by waiting in love just as the new world is waiting to be born. And then the God of all readiness says "Now!" and a world springs into being.

- John Killinger, *Christ In The Seasons of Ministry*
(Word Books,1983), 23-37.

How do you deal with crises in your life? Do you have a tendency to want to get even or to make someone hurt in a way you have been hurt? Is it possible to transform feelings of revenge into actions of blessing and have the joy of being there when "the God of all readiness says 'Now!' and a world springs into being"?

PRAYER: Forgiving Lord, so often I need help of overcoming anger and hurt feelings. May your love touch me with the grace I need to cleanse my life of dark thoughts and become a vessel of your blessing, Amen.

SATURDAY, THE FIFTH WEEK OF LENT: HOME TO BETHANY

SCRIPTURE: **John 12:1-8 Mary Anoints Jesus**

Mary took a pound of costly perfume made of pure nard, anointed Jesus' feet, and wiped them with her hair. The house was filled with the fragrance of the perfume.

Mark 14:1-9 "She Has Done What She Could."

Jesus said, "Let her alone; why do you trouble her?...She has done what she could; she has anointed my body beforehand for the burial." Truly I tell you, wherever the good news is proclaimed in the whole world, what she has done will be told in remembrance of her."

MEDITATION: A Love Gift

The journey toward Jerusalem was a lonely and challenging road in spite of the intimate relation with his Abba Father. "Foxes have holes and birds of the air have nests but the son of man has nowhere to lay his head." It was not surprising that Jesus, like the rest of us, had a strong need for home. There was one place where he seemingly felt that at-homeness. That was with Mary, Martha, and Lazarus in Bethany. John places his visit there on Saturday before the triumphal entry into Jerusalem. The disciples and close friends were there and, of course, Mary, Martha, and Lazarus. While they were still sitting at table, Mary took a pound of costly perfume and anointed Jesus and the house was filled with fragrance. The others there, particularly Judas, were very critical of such extravagance. They still did not know what was really happening. How much Mary knew we don't know, but she had the intuition that the master she deeply loved was in need. What could she do? As Jesus said, "She did what she could and for that she will be forever remembered." How this small gesture must have warmed the heart of Jesus and given him strength. Was it extravagant? Is a love gift ever extravagant? So many times with our friends we cannot suffer their sufferings or walk the lonely walk that is theirs, but we can stand by in support. "She has done what she could," said Jesus. Often that is enough.

Velma Ruch

Seizing the Moment

There is a certain extravagance in love. The alabaster phial of perfume was meant to be used drop by drop; it was meant to last for years, perhaps even for a life-time; but in a moment of utter devotion the woman poured it on the head of Jesus. Love does not stop nicely to calculate the less or more; love does not stop to work out how little it can respectably give. With a kind of divine extravagance love gives everything it has, and never counts the cost. Calculation is never any part of love.

Love knows well that there are certain moments in life which come and which do not return. There were endless and limitless opportunities to help the poor, but, if that woman had not seized that moment to make known her love to Jesus, the opportunity would never have come again. There are moments in life which do not come a second time. Impulses to devotion, impulses to reformation, impulses to decision enter the heart, and, if they are not acted on at once, they may never return. Love is ever ready to seize the moment to declare itself.

Love puts into the world a fragrance which time cannot obliterate. To this day the story of that woman's devotion moves the heart. A lovely deed is not only a thing of the moment; it leaves something in the world which time cannot take away. Love adds a permanent legacy of loveliness to life.

William Barclay, *The Mind of Jesus*
(HarperCollins, 1976), 199.

PRAYER: Lord, help us to be aware of the opening for actions that may come only once. May it never be said of us as Jesus said of Jerusalem, "If you, even you had only recognized on this day the things that make for peace, but now they are hidden from your eyes." Always, O God, give us eyes to see and ears to hear. Amen.

HOLY WEEK
THEME: THE PASSION

PALM SUNDAY HOLY WEEK
SHOUT HOSANNA

SCRIPTURE: **Luke 19:28-40 The Triumphal Entry**
Luke 19:41-44 Jesus Weeps Over Jerusalem

MEDITATION: Hosanna to the Son of David

On Palm Sunday when Jesus made his triumphal entry in Jerusalem riding on a donkey, a symbol of peace, many thought it was the Messiah for whom they had waited so long. They spread palms before him and called out:

Hosanna to the Son of David.
Blessed is he who comes in the name of the Lord.
Hosanna in highest heaven.

Not all the people could fathom what was going on. Innocent bystanders kept asking, "Who is this? Who is this?" The answer they got was "This is the prophet Jesus from Nazareth" or "This is the one who raised Lazarus from the dead." Even the closest disciple, those who had walked with Jesus for some time were among those calling out "Hosanna to the son of David" but they didn't really have much of a clue to what was going on. The writer of the Gospel of John comments, "His disciples did not understand these things at first, but when Jesus was glorified then they remembered that these things had been written of him and had been done to him" (John 12:16).

Many of us are like that as well. We have heard the stories and can recite them but what do they mean to us? We remember stories of Jesus' birth and his experience in the temple at the age of twelve: "Did you not know that I must be about my Father's business?" Then followed the unknown years until the age of thirty when he came to the river Jordan to be baptized by John. The heavens opened and the Spirit of God descended like a dove and alighted on him. And a voice from heaven said, "This is my Son, the Beloved, in whom I am well pleased." Then he was led into the wilderness where for forty days he was tempted and tested and asked the probing question, What does it mean to be Jesus?

Who am I? What did I come to do and how must I live? Jesus learned much during those forty days and when later he returned to his home town of Nazareth he was ready to make a public declaration of his mission. From Isaiah he read, "The Spirit of God is upon me for he has anointed me to bring good news." He finished by saying, "Today has this scripture been fulfilled in your hearing." Not all liked what they heard and were ready to hurl him off a cliff. Others, we are told, clung to his words.

What were these words which for awhile so enchanted the people and still move us?

They were words of love: *"I give you a new commandment that you love one another. Just as I have loved you, you also should love one another. By this every one will know you are my disciples if you have love for one another."*

They were words of forgiveness: *"Neither do I condemn you. Go and sin no more."*

They were words of healing: *"Your faith has made you whole."*

They were words of peace: *"My peace I leave with you. My peace I give you. I do not give as the world gives. Do not let your hearts be troubled and do not let them be afraid."*

They were words of salvation: *"I am the way, the truth and the life. Whoever believes in me shall not perish but have everlasting life."*

Velma Ruch

How do these words of Jesus impact your life? What would have been your thoughts as a bystander as you watched Jesus on the donkey passing by?

PRAYER: **Palm Sunday**

O God, we are like the people of Jerusalem so long ago.
We are hungry for a hero.
We crave some glimpse of greatness.
We are starving for the spectacular.
We are gathered here like those who watched
the Passion-Parade in Jerusalem,
craning our necks to catch a glimpse of our Messiah.
As we wait here for the Savior to come
let us not be disappointed when the special one appears,
even though we are certain to be surprised;
and give us courage to follow
where the one on the donkey might lead us. Amen.

Ruth C. Duck and Maren C. Tirabassi, eds. *Touch Holiness*
(The Pilgrim Press, 1900), 64.

MONDAY, HOLY WEEK
JESUS IN THE TEMPLE

SCRIPTURE: **Mark 11:15-19 Jesus and the Money Changers**
Mark 12:41-44 The Widow's Mite
Matthew 21:14-17 The Blind and the Lame Came

MEDITATION: The Money Changers and the Widow

Upon entering the Temple, Jesus sees crowds of people, pilgrims from many different countries standing in line, waiting to pay the Temple tax, Jews and converts to Jewish faith were required to pay one half-shekel around the time of the Passover. Jesus notes how the money changers charge a fee for this service, up to two-thirds of a working man's wage, and knows that worshippers from a distance especially could be exploited.

Moved by compassion for the poor who come to pray and worship, and filled with love for all who seek God in this great court, Jesus moves with holy anger against those who place a stumbling block in the way of these children of God. He wades into the rows of tables, driving our vendors who sell doves and overturning the tables of the money changers. Then he turns and refuses access to persons carrying supplies across this holy space, saying, "Is it not written, 'My house shall be called a house of prayer for all the nations'? But you have made it a den of robbers?"

In this moving act of advocacy Jesus reclaims this space for prayerful presence and directs our attention to who we are and in whose presence we gather when we enter sacred space.

* * * *

Our gospel companions lead us to another location within the Temple, the Women's Court. Jesus is observing people as they place money in the Temple treasury there. Many rich people give large sums. Then a very poor widow walks by and throws in two mites (worth about two-fifths of a cent,) prompting Jesus to say:

> *This poor widow has put in more than all those who are contributing to the treasury. For all of them have contributed out of their abundance; but she out of her poverty has put in everything she had, all she had to live on*
>
> (Mark 12:43-44).

This woman stands at the opposite end of the socioeconomic line from the rich in her ability to contribute financially, but in the eyes of God she has given more than all the others. Spiritual direction helps us notice how following Jesus turns our economics upside down and shakes the contents out onto the floor of God's presence.. . .Jesus, too, has lived as a poor person with no income other than what is given him, and no place to live other than what others offer. Jesus has lived in simple trust in Abba and in others. Now he is about to give himself: all he has.

Wendy J. Miller, *Jesus Our Spiritual Director*
(Upper Room Books, 2004), 159-161.

Giving All

It makes no difference at all, God be praised how great or how small the task may be. In relation to the highest of all this simply does not matter when it comes to being willing to do all...All the ruinous quarreling and comparison which swells up and injures, which sighs and envies, the Eternal does not recognize....The demand upon each is exactly the same: to be willing to do all. If this be fulfilled then the Good bestows its blessing equally upon each one who makes and remains loyal to his commitment. (125).

A person may say, "I have not the strength to risk all." Again an evasion by the aid of the word "all." For the Good is quite capable of reckoning and computing its demand in relation to the strength that this [person] has. And what is more, if he will venture in all sincerity, then he will certainly receive strength enough in the act of decision. But the clever one desires by the help of evasions to have strength in advance. . Yet it is also certain that the one who does not have trust does not receive this strength. Look, the great battleship first gets its orders when it is far out at sea, the little sloop knows all in advance. And in a spiritual sense, a person is only really out at sea who is willing to do all, irrespective of whether he is the highest or the least. ...The widow's mite was all that she owned. Before God it was as great a sum as all of the world's gold in a single heap.

. . . Yet when the public collection of money was made, it was possible that the collectors both kindly and politely might have said to the widow, "No, Mother, you keep your mite." But the Good – how shall we express it? Its goodness is so great, that it recognizes no difference.

Soren Kierkegaard, *Purity of Heart Is To Will One Thing*, Douglas V. Steere, trans. (Harper and Brothers Publishers, 1948), 129-130.

The Blind and the Lame Came to Him

We could recount story after story of how an encounter with Jesus changed lives. The remarkable thing is that these encounters did not just take place in the few short years of Jesus' ministry here on earth. They continue through Christ's presence in our lives. Sometimes we may be Zaccheus up in the tree longing for something or someone to straighten out twisted lives. Sometimes we may be the blind Bartimeus sitting by the road calling out, "Jesus, Son of David, have mercy on me." "What do you want," said Jesus. "Lord, I want to see." Or the woman bent over for eighteen years who did not know what it meant to stand upright. She just could look at the ground. Sometimes we, too, forget what it means to stand upright and look into the face of Christ. We may think the dirt around our feet is all there is.

The love of Jesus revealed to us in these experiences is a gift. It does not depend on how worthy we may be or not be, but for it to make a difference in our lives and the lives of others, there is a price. We must pay attention. We must heighten our awareness of the Divine in all things. We must open our lives to that presence. We must experience the sacrament of the present moment or what has been called every-day sacredness. Such awareness of the presence of the Divine in life's minutiae does not happen automatically. It takes practice. It means being called to remembrance, but what can be better than living each day knowing that the love of Christ is radiant in our lives in every moment.

The experiences and teachings of Jesus in the Temple have great meaning for us today. What have you learned from the story of the money changers and the widow's mite? What does it mean "to give all"? Is that possible for you? Have you ever found yourself figuratively among the lame and the blind?

Velma Ruch

PRAYER: Prayer of the Lame

O Lord my God, I called to you
or help and you healed me.
(Psalm 30:2 NIV)

Lord of the lame, I cannot even beg
My tongue has been severed by doubt
Hands once raised toward you,
knees once bent before you
are withered from lack of use.

Lord of the lowest, Lord of the least,
I am blind as the blind you cured.
I am as mute and as deaf.
My only possession is hope
in your healing power.

Fill me with Spirit! Define me with form!
Raise up the flesh of my faith!
Transformed by your touch and your breath,
I will walk with you, speak for you,
see things anew, listen always for you.
O Lord, listen always for you.
Amen.

Phyllis Price, *Holy Fire*

TUESDAY, HOLY WEEK
THE GREEKS

SCRIPTURE: John 12:20-36 "We Would See Jesus"

MEDITATION: "But for This Cause Came I Unto This Hour"

In the week we know as Holy Week, Jesus spent much of his time in the Temple. There were some difficult times. One of those occurred probably on Tuesday, when some Greeks approached and said, "We would see Jesus." Here was Jesus recognizing he was probably in the Temple for the last time, the Temple where as a child he had felt the call to be about his Father's business. One cannot blame him if he wondered what had become of it all. What were the fruits of a sacrificial life? Could there have been a momentary temptation for him to forget the Jews and Gethsemane and the cross. The priests would have been glad for him to take off so they wouldn't have to deal with him. The disciples wanted him to take the safe course. Rationalization would have been so easy. Why not go with the Greeks? I could do more good teaching them than staying here and dying. The scriptures indicate a brief turmoil within Christ at this moment. As one wrote about it, "One of death's icy windblasts blew over his heart and he said, 'Now is my soul troubled, and what shall I say?'" It was like a moment of Gethsemane before Gethsemane. And what shall I say? What can one say at such times? "Let me escape. Must this cup be mine?" "Father," prayed Christ, "save me from this hour." Never before had Christ said anything like this, but now his heart was troubled. It didn't last long. "But for this cause came I unto this hour. Father, glorify thy name." Having reaffirmed his decision the Spirit came in confirming power. "I have both glorified it and will glorify it again." Jesus could have saved his life but it would have meant the sacrifice of all he had stood for. It would have stripped his life of meaning. The turning away was only momentary and the assurance from his father was unmistakable. "You have already glorified my name. Your work is acceptable to me. Have courage for its completion."

Velma Ruch

We Would See Jesus

We would see Jesus! Lo, his star is shining
Above the stable where the angels sing.
There in a manger on the hay reclining
Haste, let us lay our gifts before the King.

We would see Jesus on the mountain teaching
With all the listening people gathered round.
While birds and flowers and sky above are preaching
The blessedness which simple trust has found.

We would see Jesus in his work of healing
At eventide before the sun was set.
Divine and human in his deep revealing
Of God and humankind in service met.
We would see Jesus; in the early morning
Still as of old he calls us "Follow me"
Let us arise, all lesser service scorning,
Lord, we are thine, we give ourselves to thee!

J. Edgar Park, *Hymns of the Saints,* # 217

WEDNESDAY, HOLY WEEK
REST AND BETRAYAL

SCRIPTURE: **Matthew 26:1-5, 14-16 Plans for Betrayal**

MEDITATION: Paid to Betray

The hurricane is forming now. Two days before the Passover festival the chief priests and scribes meet in the palace of the high priest to discuss how they can arrest Jesus secretly and have him killed. In collusion with the dark forces at work within the religious leaders, Satan is also infiltrating the life of Judas Iscariot, who meets with the chief priest and the Temple police to plan the betrayal of Jesus. Happy with Judas's cooperation, the religious leaders agree to pay him money for his services; the deal is made. . . . Judas begins to seek an opportunity for the religious leaders to arrest Jesus, a time when the crowds would not see or know what was happening.

Wendy J. Miller, *Jesus Our Spiritual Director*, 163.

The Kiss

{Who gave the kiss of betrayal to Jesus}? It was Judas Iscariot. Though little is actually known about Judas and his motivation, legend invests his character with a perhaps unwarranted , definitive degree of evil. Dante, for example, places Judas in the pit of hell, at the lowest level of degradation. Along with the traitors Brutus and Cassius, he depicts Judas dangling from one of the mouths of Satan. Others, somewhat more benevolently suggest that Judas, as a member of the Zealots, was disappointed in Jesus and with a miscalculated hope of forcing Jesus to action, collaborated with the enemy. The deeper truth does not lie in making Judas the personification of evil, nor in justifying his actions and thereby excusing him of responsibility. The human personality is too complex for such simplistic judgments.

We cannot underestimate, however, the significance of the person of Judas, his presence and action, at this juncture in Jesus' life. Moreover, Judas' character and actions mirror the potential for evil and betrayal that stalks our own inner darkness. Judas betrayal of Jesus brings us face to face with the dark side of our selves. Examining it challenges us to a greater awareness of how we betray our God, ourselves, and each other.

Bergan and Schwan, *Surrender: A Guide for Prayer*
(St. Mary's Press, 1986) 66.

It isn't comfortable for us to identify ourselves with Judas, but can we understand Judas perhaps a little better when we penetrate into the depths of some of our own actions? What are the things in our lives for which we need to be forgiven?

PRAYER: We pray, "Forgive us our trespasses as we forgive those who trespass against us." May we, O God, be equal to recognizing our own trespasses and the depth of love that allows us to forgive others, we pray. Amen

Thursday, Holy Week
MAUNDY THURSDAY

SCRIPTURE: **Luke 22:7-13 Preparation for Passover**
John 13:1-17 A Towel and a Basin
1 Cor. 11:23-26 Eat this Bread; Drink This Cup
Matthew 26:36-46 Gethsemane

MEDITATION: Eat This Bread, Drink This Cup

Thursday locates us around the time of the Jewish Passover in Jerusalem where Jesus and his disciples have gathered in an upper room. The events leading up to his impending arrest have already taken place. . . . All of the Gospel narratives are heavy with a sense of impending doom. Jesus feels the precariousness of his position. Indeed, his highly visible entry into the city, with the climate of the city as tense as it was, could only have been made with Jesus fully conscious of the inflammatory consequences of such an act. He knows too that his present whereabouts will be made known to officials by one of his own number.

It is at this tense moment that Jesus enacts two distinctive gestures that will become symbolic of the entirety of his teaching and be ritually recapitulated over and over by Christian communities of succeeding generations. The gestures are at once utterly simple and profound, speaking, as only gestures can, more eloquently than the most polished words. He washes his friends' feet, and he shares a meal.

The two central gestures of the liturgy for Maundy Thursday are intimately connected. Both speak nonverbally of nurturing. I begin first with the gesture through which this is most obviously communicated:

> *[The] Lord Jesus on the night when he was betrayed took bread, and when he had given thanks, he broke it, and said, "This is my body which is for you. Do this in remembrance of me." In the same way also the cup, after supper, saying, "This cup is the new covenant in my blood. Do this, as often as you drink it, in remembrance of me.*
>
> 1 Corinthians 11:23-25.

To break bread and pass the cup became, for the earliest Christians the ritual gesture that defined who they were. . . . At its most elemental level, the gesture proclaims Christianity as a community of mutual need and nourishment whose very life, at all its levels, is sustained by its continuous feeding of one another and being fed, a nurturant symbiosis constantly replenished by the nourishment of Christ's own sustenance.

Holy Thursday is the day on which the Christian community in a special way celebrates Christ's maternal nurturance. It is also the day on which we are enjoined to nurture one another, to love as we have been loved. With a mother's tender love we are entrusted to each other. We eat from the same table. We drink from the same cup. We give to each other from our own substance. We, in turn, are fed by one another. The sharing we do in the church, the body of Christ, is more than fellowship, more than working side by side. We share in a profound communion at the root of our beings, on levels only dimly accessible to consciousness. We are lives interconnected at the core.

The foot washing is a wonderfully pregnant ritual full of import for the day in which our mutuality is as much in focus. . . . In the gospel account Jesus is quite explicit about the gesture's meaning. This is a new command. Love a new way. Love by caretaking. Love by being available to one another. Love by serving. In a world which clamors for status and recognition, this is a countercultural statement.

Wendy M. Wright, *The Rising*,
(Upper Room Books, 1994), 86-90.

Gethsemane

The struggle within Jesus in the garden of Gethsemane was so intense that he sweat drops of blood. He prayed, "Father, if it is possible, let this cup pass from me." But then, as with the Greeks, he let go in trust and prayed, "Yet not my will but thine be done." Henri Nouwen in his book Can You Drink the Cup? asks, How could Jesus say yes? "In his immense loneliness, Jesus fell on his face and cried, 'My Father, if it is possible, let this cup pass me by.' Jesus couldn't face it. Too much pain to hold, too much suffering to embrace, too much agony to live through. ...Why, then, could he still say yes? I can't fully answer that question, except to say that beyond all the abandonment experienced in body and mind Jesus still had a spiritual bond with the one he called Abba. He possessed a trust beyond betrayal, a surrender beyond despair, love beyond all fears. This intimacy beyond all human intimacies made it possible for Jesus to allow the request to let the cup pass him by become a prayer directed to the one who had called him, 'My beloved.'....It was that spiritual sinew, that intimate communion with his Father that made him hold on to the cup and pray, 'My Father, let it be as you, not I would have it.'" (36-37).

A Sacrament

At the 1988 World Conference, Anne Welch, who dealt in crisis ministries in Independence, Missouri, told of an experience when one of the hospital chaplains came to her and said, "I have just participated in a sacrament, but I don't know what to call it." He told of visiting with a young woman who was terminally ill with cancer. She talked to him for two hours about how much she wanted to live – about her children who needed a mother, about her husband who depended on her, about the many things she desired to do that she had not yet accomplished. There was agony in the telling. Then there was a long pause and a great peace came over her and she said, "But if God wants me, he can have me." It was not resignation. It was a deliberate gift of her life to God. After listening to this story, Anne said quietly, "The name of your sacrament is Gethsemane. You were awake to what the disciples slept through."

Velma Ruch, *Summoned to Pilgrimage*, 90-91.

Gethsemane

All paths that have been or shall be
Pass somewhere through Gethsemane.
All those who journey soon or late
Must pass within that garden gate,
Must kneel alone in darkness there
And battle with some fierce despair.
God pity those who cannot say,

"Not mine, but thine," who only pray,
"Let this cup pass," and cannot see
The Purpose in Gethsemane.

Ella Wheeler Wilcox

Can you drink the cup that is your cup? Are you willing to accept the pain your discipleship may cost you? Are you ready to be generous with your commitment even if it brings suffering your way? In other words, are you willing to walk in the footsteps of Jesus?

PRAYER: Loving God, I so much want to say yes to those questions but I know my own weakness and am not sure I can follow you all the way. Accept my weakness and transform my deep desires into strength through the power of the Holy Spirit, I pray. Amen

FRIDAY, HOLY WEEK
GOOD FRIDAY

SCRIPTURE: **John 18:1-12 "Whom Do You Seek?"**
John 19:16-30 The Crucifixion
Luke 23:32-43 "Remember Me When You Come Into Your Kingdom."

MEDITATION: "Whom Do You Seek?"

Jesus emerges from the Garden of Gethsemane after his agonizing ordeal in prayer, sweaty from the struggle. But the heart that was poured out so emotionally is now filled with resolve to drink the cup set before him. No matter how bitter. No matter how difficult to swallow . . . . .

Through the grove comes the muted clatter of what sounds like a mob. Torches bob above the crowd, curling plumes of black smoke into the night. As the disciples squint through the gnarled silhouettes of the trees, they discover that the mob is comprised of military men....The detachment numbers about six hundred men.

How ironic. A detachment of soldiers coming for the One who could, with a whispered prayer, deploy legions of angels for his defense. How very ironic. Coming for the light of the world with torches and lanterns. Coming with hand-crafted swords and clubs for the one who forged the stars. . . .

Jesus steps forward. Courageously. Resolutely. An unarmed man squared off against a small army. He is the first to speak: "Who is it you want?" The reply is crisp as the night air. "Jesus the Nazarene." Without hesitation or a ploy to cloak his identity, Jesus answers, "I am he.". . . .At the words, "I am," the soldiers collapse. In one brief but incredible display of deity, Jesus over powers his opposition.. . . .

Again Jesus asks who they are looking for. Again they reply. Again he identifies himself. But this time he includes a plea for his disciples, "If you are looking for me, then let these men go."

Judas then steps from the shadows to point out Jesus to his captors. And he does so, deceitfully, with a kiss. "Friend," Jesus says to him, "Do what you came for." The servant of the high priest advances to take Jesus into custody. As he does, Peter whips out his sword and takes a swing at the man. The servant jerks his head out of the way, but the sword manages to sever part of his ear.....Jesus turns his attention to the servant cupping his ear. He touches the wound. Immediately it is healed.

Luke is the only gospel writer to document the healing. Maybe to the others the miracle seemed minuscule in light of the tragedy being enacted before them. After all, of what consequence is the earlobe of a servant when the Savior of the world's life is at stake?

It was the last miracle Jesus performed before he died. And the smallest...Maybe it wasn't such a small miracle after all. In light of the legions of angels at his disposal and in light of how the Savior could have used his power, maybe, just maybe, it was his greatest.

From Ken Gire, *Incredible Moments With The Savior*
(Daybreak Books, 1990), 111-113

The Cross and the Shadow

One day as in meditation I walked the Worshipers' Path in the Temple, I came to the shadow of the cross. It captivated me. I walked to inspect the cross more closely. After a while I turned around and with my back to the cross was startled to see my

shadow super-imposed on the shadow of the cross. I experienced a momentary shudder of fear. I wasn't sure I was prepared for what that meant. Almost immediately, however, I felt as if the stark arms of the cross softened and enfolded me in love. It was with joy I continued my journey into the light and beauty and preparatory cleansing of becoming part of the redeemed community for which Christ died.

The cross to me, perhaps more than the resurrection is so representative of the life of Jesus. Amid mocking cries of "Save yourself. Save yourself," Jesus no doubt remembered how at times he had wanted to do just that. It happened in the wilderness after his baptism. It happened when some Greeks offered him the opportunity to go with them. It happened in the Garden of Gethsemane. Each time he was true to his vocation and chose the difficult way. Now here he was hanging on the cross, surrounded by voices of derision. Then suddenly in the midst of it all there came the quiet voice of a desperate man hanging at his side, "Jesus, remember me when you come into your kingdom." "Today you shall be with me in paradise," came the response. We wonder how many times since, the desperate and lonely ones of the world have come with the same request and found themselves accepted.

Then there was John, the beloved disciple, standing at the foot of the cross. He was once known as Boanerges, one of the Sons of Thunder. Once he had wanted Jesus to call down fire on the Samaritans, who had not accepted Jesus. Now here was this same Jesus saying, "Forgive them. Forgive them for they know not what they do." The disciple whom Jesus loved learned that day something of the price of love.

Before breathing his last, Jesus said, "It is finished" or as it is translated in Danish, *"Det er fullbragt"* – "It is fulfilled." Victory is won. About this the Danish philosopher Soren Kierkegaard has written, "'It is finished,' he said, nailed to the cross as he was at the very time when his mother stood there – as if nailed to the cross by horror at this sight...And yet, eternally understood the crucified one had in the same moment accomplished all. With eternity's wisdom [he said], 'It is finished.'"

And it was. The dream had taken hold. In a world of violence and suffering and injustice there is transforming love that will not let the dream die. I was touched by that love that day in the Temple. Though my expression of it has been imperfect. I cannot forget. Neither can you.

Velma Ruch, "The Cross and the Shadow,"
Herald, April 2004, 16.

"It Is Finished"

. . . The view of the moment is the opinion which in an earthly and busy sense decides whether a man accomplishes anything or not. And in this sense, nothing in the world has ever been so completely lost as was Christianity at the time that Christ was crucified. And in the understanding of the moment, never in the world has anyone accomplished so little by the sacrifice of a consecrated life as did Jesus Christ. And yet in this same instant, eternally understood, he had accomplished all. ...Eternally understood, the crucified one had in the same moment accomplished all.. . . and on that account said, with eternity's wisdom, "It is finished."

For it is not after the passage of eighteen hundred years that He will now again appear, and referring to the outcome, say, "It is finished." In contrast to this, he would still not say that. Perhaps it would require many centuries before he would be able to say that in regard to temporal existence. Yet what he is still unable to say after the passage of eighteen triumphant centuries, he said in his own age, eighteen centuries ago, in the moment when all was lost. Eternally understood, he said, "It is finished." "It is finished," he said that just when the mass of the people, and the priests, and the Roman soldiers, Herod and Pilate, and the idle ones on the street, the crowd in the gateway, and the newspaper reporters, (if there were any such at that time) in short, when all the powers of the moment, however different their sentiments might have been, were agreed upon this view of the matter; that all was lost, hopelessly lost. "It is finished," he said, nailed to the cross as he was, at the very time when his mother stood there – as if nailed to the cross, when his disciples' eyes were as if nailed to the cross by horror at this sight. Hence motherhood and faithfulness submitted to the moment's view of the matter, that all was lost. Oh, then let us by this most horrible thing, which once took place (and that it happened only once is not to the world's credit, but rather that the crucified one is eternally and essentially different from every other man), let us learn wisdom in the lesser relationships. Let us never deceive youth by foolish talk about the matter of accomplishing. Let us never make them busy in the service of the moment, instead of in patience willing something eternal. Let us not make them quick to judge what they perhaps do not understand, instead of willing something eternal and being content with little for themselves! Let us rightly consider that a generation is not on that account superior because it understands that a previous generation acted wrongly, if in the present moment they themselves do not understand how to discriminate between the momentary and the eternal aspect of the thing at hand,

Soren Kierkegaard, *Purity of Heart Is To Will One Thing*, Douglas V. Steere, trans. (New York: Harper and Brothers Publishers, 1948) 137-139.

Pilate Remembers

I wonder why that scene comes back tonight,
That long forgotten scene of years ago;
Perhaps this touch of spring, that full, white moon,
For it was spring and spring's white moon hung low
Above my garden the night he died.
I still remember how I felt disturbed
That I must send him to a felon's cross
On such a day when spring was in the air
And in his life, for he was young to die.
How tall and strong he stood, how calm his eyes,
Fronting me straight and while I questioned him
His fearless heart spoke to me through his eyes.
Could I have won him as my follower
And a hundred more beside, my way had let
To Caesar's palace and I'd wear today
The imperial purple. But he would not move
One little bit from his wild madcap dream
Of seeking truth. What wants a man with truth
When he is young and spring is at the door?

He would not listen so he had to go.
One mad Jew less meant little to the state
And pleasing Annas made my task the less.
And yet for me he spoiled that silver night –
Remembering it was spring and he was young.

William E. Brooks

PRAYER: **Savior, Thy Dying Love**

Savior, thy dying love, Thou gavest me
Nor should I aught withhold, Dear Lord, from thee.
In love my soul would bow, by heart fulfill its vow,
Some offering bring thee now, Something for thee.

Give me a faithful heart, Likeness to thee,
That each departing day Henceforth may see
Some work of love begun, Some deed of kindness done,
Some wanderer sought and won, Something for thee.

All that I am and have, Thy gifts so free,
Ever in joy or grief, My Lord, for thee;
And when thy face I see, My ransomed soul shall be
Through all eternity Something for thee. Amen.

S. Dryden Phelps, *Hymns of the Saints*, # 442.

SATURDAY, HOLY WEEK
THE SABBATH — STILLNESS

SCRIPTURE: **John 19:31-42 None of His Bones Shall Be Broken**
Luke 23:50-56 Joseph of Arimathea
Isaiah 53 The Suffering Servant

MEDITATION: Joseph of Arimathea

There is a certain tragedy about Joseph of Arimathea. He is the man who gave Jesus a tomb. He was a member of the Sanhedrin; we are told that he did not agree with the verdict and the sentence of that court. But there is no word that he raised his voice in disagreement. Maybe he kept silent; maybe he absented himself when he saw that he was powerless to stop a course of action with which he disagreed. What a difference it would have made if he had spoken! How it would have lifted up Jesus' heart if in that grim assembly of bleak hatred, even one lone voice had spoken for him! But Joseph waited until Jesus was dead, and then he gave him a tomb. It is one of the tragedies of life that we place on people's graves the flowers we might have given them when they were alive. We keep for their obituary notices and for the tributes paid to them at memorial services and in committee minutes, the praise and thanks we should have given them when they lived. Often, often we are haunted because we never spoke. A word to the living is worth a cataract of tributes to the dead.

William Barclay, *The Gospel of Luke*
(The Westminster Press, 1975) 290.

As Sabbath begins, the women rest and wait. Their vigil continues. The other disciples hide in a locked room, fearing for their lives.

Wendy Miller

Have you recognized yourself in any of the disciples surrounding Jesus at the time of the crucifixion? What would you have done had you been there?

The Suffering Servant

The earliest and probably the most profound statement on human suffering in all of literature is the Song of the Suffering Servant found in the book of Isaiah. In his writing Isaiah, one of the greatest prophets and poets of the Jewish scriptures brought to the Jewish people a message of their deliverance from bondage by a God of tender compassion. It is a message of hope for a displaced people who have undergone the total collapse of their nation, the loss of their religious center, and utter homelessness in a land of exile. In words that transcend his own time and nation, Isaiah attempted to lead his people to discover, within their suffering, a new meaning that would carry them into the future.

The song depicts an ideal servant of God. The role of the servant is to liberate others by willingly and consciously taking upon himself or herself their pain, sin, and suffering.

Jesus consistently identifies with and lived out of the spirit of the suffering servant of Isaiah (Mark 8:31; Matt. 17:22-23).

As beloved Son of God Jesus provides us, the people of the Christian scriptures, with the model for suffering and the means of true servanthood through his life, his cross and his resurrection.

Jaqueline Syrup Bergan and Marie Schwan, *Surrender: A Guide for Prayer* (Saint Mary's Press, 1986), 133.

In regard to your own life, what stands out for you in Jesus' life, death, and resurrection?

PRAYER: Eternal God, Our Savior and Redeemer, we kneel in awe as we contemplate your great love for us. We have participated in the darkness of those who lost you on the cross and anticipate with joy the coming resurrection. May our life and servanthood be a reflection of your love as we grow in our discipleship, we pray. Amen

EASTER
RESURRECTION

EASTER SUNDAY
HE LIVES FOR WE HAVE SEEN HIM

SCRIPTURE: **Matthew 18:1-10 Resurrection of Jesus**
John 20:11-18 Mary Magdalene
D. and C. 76:3g-h He Lives, For We Have Seen Him

Meditation: Christ Is Risen Indeed

We awoke this morning as we do every morning to the living presence of the risen Christ. What a marvel that is and what a source of joy. "Now is Christ risen from the dead." Now, now. And that now is forever. What a transformation it would make in our lives if we never forgot that fact for a moment, if it lived in our consciousness always. Resurrection is the word of transformation, but it has a price. We must change our lives. As we read the scriptures we are struck by the staggering nature of the rewards promised to those who are willing to undergo the discipline of Christ-like living. It seems our Lord finds our desires not too strong but too weak. We are half-hearted creatures, often fooling around with tinsel when we could have gold, with the glitter of the temporary when we could have the glory of the eternal. The eternal is not just for some after life. It is for now. "This is life eternal that ye know me the only true and living God and Jesus Christ whom I have sent."

Mary Magdalene

Early on the first day of the week – while it was still dark – Mary Magdalene came to the tomb and saw that the stone had been moved from the tomb. She had spent all day Friday standing at the foot of the cross watching her friend and Savior die. Now she thought that the body had been stolen. In confusion and fear she ran to tell the other disciples. Peter and John came running, but this time John outran Peter and got there first. John looked in the tomb, saw the linen wrappings, but dashed right in. That gave John courage to follow. The scripture says, "He saw and believed." It did not say what he believed. It is possible that the very same John about whom this story is told is also the John who is narrating this event. He comments that the disciples did not yet understand that Christ would rise from the dead so they just left and went home.

Mary Magdalene, however stayed, but even though she saw two angels in the tomb she believed the body had been stolen. Then she heard a voice behind her saying, "Why are you crying?" I have always thought it significant that the first recorded words of Jesus after the resurrection were, "Why are you crying?" It shows such a concern for our pain, confusion and disorientation. Mary did not have the expectation of seeing Jesus, just the gardener. Then she heard her name, "Mary" and she knew and responded, "Rabbouni." She received the commission, "Go tell" and thus was the first to give the marvelous news of the resurrection.

Probably most of us at some time in our lives have had an experience not too dissimilar from Mary. Like the disciples on the road to Emmaus we find our dreams shattered, we experience pain and disorientation, and the way before us is obscured. In the midst of that darkness and despair a voice penetrates our very being, "My child, why are you crying?" and life is made new again. We are whole once more. The journey ahead may still be difficult but we are accompanied by the God who once said through Isaiah, "I have called you by name, you are mine. When you pass through the waters, I will be with you; and through the rivers, they shall not overwhelm you; when you walk through fire you shall not be burned and the flame shall not consume you. For I am the Lord your God, the Holy One of Israel, your Savior.

Velma Ruch

"Peace Be With You"

(John 20: 19-23)

...Jesus himself was suddenly standing there among them.
He said, "Peace be with you."
But the whole group was terribly frightened,
thinking they were seeing a ghost!
"Why are you frightened?" he asked
"Why do you doubt who I am?
Look at my hands. Look at my feet,
you can see that it's really me.
Touch me and make sure that I am not a ghost,
because ghosts don't have bodies, as you see that I do!"
As he spoke, he held out his hands for them to see,
and he showed them his feet.
Still they stood there doubting, filled with joy and wonder.
Then he asked them, "Do you have anything here to eat?"
They gave him a piece of broiled fish, and he ate it as they watched.

(from *TouchPoint Bible*)

Peace Be With You

When Christ died on the tree of the cross, all the hopes and dreams of the disciples were shattered. Their courageous zeal yielded to fear and listlessness. Their confidence gave way to disbelief and doubt. Locked, indeed, in their own powerlessness, the disciples were dispirited. It was as if when Jesus died they lost their soul. Where had it all gone?

"Peace be with you."

Jesus enters through the locked door of the disciples' hearts. He pierces their fear and seizes hold of them. In his presence the walls of their confinement tumble. This is Jesus of Nazareth! He stands before them, risen in power yet bearing his wounds. Transfixed by his risen presence, the disciples are delivered into enthralling ecstatic joy!

He had promised his beloved disciples at their last meal together that he would return. He had promised that he would bring them a peace that would heal and strengthen them beyond their most cherished dreams. Now he is before them. "Peace be with you.". . . .

The moment when the disciples were given birth has now suddenly come to fullness. Through the breath of Christ, they receive the life and power of the Spirit. The new creation has begun.

Jaqueline Syrup Bergan and S. Marie Schwan,*Freedom: A Guide to Prayer*
(St. Mary's Press, 1988), 68-69.

Jesus and Thomas

(John 20: 24-29)

Like Thomas, at times, we, too, find ourselves locked in doubt, sadly refusing joy's entry into our life. This locked-in-ness is a subtle phenomenon, a gradual giving way to insecurities and self-doubt from which springs a fundamental demand for proofs and miraculous intervention. We put on blinders and say, "Show me!"

It was into the midst of the anguish and loneliness of doubt that Christ suddenly appeared to Thomas. It is in the midst of our woundedness that Christ continues to be a healing Easter presence. Amazingly, it was the blinding doubt of Thomas that served the function of making known to the world the wonder of God's merciful love. His skeptical bargaining was met with unconditional acceptance by Jesus. Jesus did not rebuke Thomas. He accepted him totally, going so far as to invite him to satisfy his appetite for proof. By putting his hand into the wound in his side, his finger into the wounds of his hands and feet, Thomas' heart was instantly overwhelmed with the awareness of the magnitude of Christ's gentleness and understanding. Pierced through with such love, Thomas knew; he knew with the knowledge of the Spirit:

"My Lord, and my God."

In his act of surrender, the wounds of doubt, like agonizing boils, are first pierced then healed by Jesus' love. Thomas became whole in the strength of conviction and commitment. Once again power was made perfect in weakness (2 Cor. 12:9).

Bergan and Schwan, *Freedom: A Guide to Prayer,* 78-79)

Christ is Risen! Alleluia!

Indeed we do have cause to celebrate. No other event in all of history is comparable to the one we celebrate today. With the Resurrection of our Lord, a new age dawned, a new chapter was written in the story of the love that God has for us. We, as Christians, should see the Resurrection not only as history. We should see in it the mystery of the redemption of humanity and our own personal transformation. The triumphant resurrection of Christ was not only the confirmation of all he said and taught during his earthly life, but also was a confirmation of his divinity, his divine authority. He had promised to conquer death and he kept that promise. That day Jesus was called to arise and come forth and he answered that call. Because he answered that call, we, in turn, are called to that same task. Like the women at the tomb and the disciples who heard the good news shortly thereafter, we are called to rise again to new life in Christ and to share that life with others. On this Easter morning, may the marvel of Christ risen bring us joy, peace, and all the blessing and inspiration we need. May we, as we have turned our hearts and minds to this powerfully familiar story experience once again the wonder of the Resurrection.

Edith Gallaher

PRAYER: Risen Redeemer, may we ever comprehend the meaning of the Resurrection and have the power to live it as we tell the story to others. Amen

Sending Forth

We have come to the end of this portion of our journey.
Let us continue in the common knowledge that we are called
to be the people of God, to participate in his mission to the world.
We are Christ's body, his caring touch and his loving embrace.
Let us center upon this moment, this day, in great expectation.
This is our time to live, to come to the God who creates us,
to sing to the Redeemer who frees us, to stand before the Spirit
who sustains us.
Breathe on us, O breath of God, and continually renew us into new life.

WORKS CITED

(The page number following each citation refers to the page number in which the quotation appears in this book).

Aldrich, Bess Streeter, *A Lantern in Her Hand.* Quoted in Rita Snowden, *I Believe Here and Now* (Great Britain: Fount Paperbacks, 1981), 79.

Auden, W. H., *For the Time Being: Collected Longer Poems* (New York: Vintage Random House, 1974), 20.

Augustine, *Confessions,* John K. Ryan, trans. (New York: Image Doubleday, 1960), 75.

Barclay, William, *The Gospel of Luke,* (Philadelphia: The Westminster Press, 1975), 91; 93; 113.
The Mind Of Jesus (Harper San Francisco, 1976), 97-98.

Bergan, Jacqueline Syrup and S. Marie Schwan, *Forgiveness: A Guide for Prayer, 64; Freedom: A Guide for Prayer, 116-117; Surrender: A Guide for Prayer* (Winona, Minnesota: St. Mary's Press, 1985), 105; 113-114.

Bonhoeffer, Dietrick, *Letters and Papers from Prison,* rev. ed. (New York: Macmillan Publishing Company, 1953, 1967, 1971), 89-90.

Book of Mormon, (Independence, Missouri: Herald Publishing House, 1966).

Brooks, William E., "Pilate Remembers," 111-112.

Brother Roger, *A Life We Never Dared Hope For.* Quoted in *Alive Now* (May/June, 1993), 88.

Buechner, Frederich, *Listening to Your Life* (Harper San Francisco, 1992). 6.
"The Road Goes On," in *A Room Called Remember* (San Francisco: Harper, 1992). 9.

Buresh, Anne Squire, "Saints Are Not Born To It," 76.

Caretto, Carlo, *Letters from the Desert* (Maryknoll, New York: Orbis, 1972), 38.

Cannato, Judy, "The Labyrinth: "Praying Psalm 139," *Weavings* (May/June 2002) 15.

Carney, Glandion and William Long, *Longing for God: Prayer & the Rhythms of Life,* (Downers Grove, Illinois: InterVarsity Press, 1993), 71.

Chisholm, Cathy Cummings, "Creative Spirit" and "Fisher of Folk," in *Landscapes of the Heart,* pp. 11 and 105. Published by Bridge Resources, 1998. Used by permission of Congregational Ministries Publishing, Presbyterian Church (U.S.A.), 100 Witherspoon St., Lousiville, KY 40202, 10; 37.

Chvala-Smith, Anthony, "Prayer in the Book of Mormon" in Velma Ruch, *Transforming Power of Prayer*, Vol. 1 (Independence, Missouri: Herald Publishing House, 1999), 81; 81-82.

Understanding the Way: Exploring Our Church's Faith (Independence, Missouri: Herald House, 2003), 51; 58; 60-61.

Companions in Christ: The Way of Forgiveness (Nashville: Upper Room, 2002), 65.

Compier, Don, "He Is Present At The Table," *Herald (February, 2005), 67-68.*

Davis, Mary Ogden, *Metanoia: A Transformational Journey* (Marina Del Ray, California: De Voss and Co., 1984). 11.

Del Bene, Ron, *The Hunger of the Heart* (Nashville: Upper Room Books, 1992), 85-86.

Doctrine and Covenants (Independence, Missouri: Herald Publishing House).

Doughty, Stephen V. "Why Are They, Well So...?" *Weavings* (May/June, 1999), 51-52; 57-58.

Duck, Ruth C. and Maren C. Tirabassi, eds. *Touch Holiness* (New York: The Pilgrim Press, 1993), 100.

Eliot, T. S. *The Rock: A Pageant Play* (London: Faber and Faber, 1934), 70-71

Forbes, James, *Preaching and the Holy Spirit* (Nashville: Arlington Press, 1989), 44.

Foster, Richard, *Prayer: Finding the Heart's True Home (*HarperSanFrancisco, 1992). 17

Streams of Living Water (HarperSanFrancisco, 1998). 23.

Gallaher, Edith. "True Fasting," and "A Time of Prayer." 13, "Christ Is Risen! Alleluia!"(unpublished), 117.

Gire, Ken, *Incredible Moments with the Savior* (Grand Rapids, Michigan: Daybreak Books, 1990), 109.

Graffeo, Everett, "Life As a Journey, " and "Spirituality." (unpublished). 3, 4.

Hammarskjold, Dag, *Markings,* Trans. From the Swedish by Leif Sjoberg and W. H. Auden (New York: Alfred A. Knopf, 1964), 34.

Heinze, David M. "The Sacramental Life," *Herald* (February, 2005), 67.

Hinsen, E. Glenn, "Reconciliation and Resistance," *Weavings* (November/December 2000), 62.

*Hymns of the Saints (*Independence, Missouri: Herald Publishing House, 1981).

Anonymous, 1880 "I Sought the Lord," # 213.

Barton, Bernard, "Walk in the Light" # 303.

Clephane, Elizabeth C. "Beneath the Cross of Jesus," # 428

Ferris, Deam, "Fountain of All Revelation," # 298..

Grant, Robert, "Father, When In Love to Thee," # 116.

Homer, Charlotte G. "Great and Marvelous Are Thy Works," # 48.
Niles, John Jacob, "I Wonder As I Wander," Appalachian Folk Carol, # 251.
Park, J. Edgar, "We Would See Jesus," # 217.
Phelps, S. Dryden, "Savior, Thy Dying Love," # 442.
Spencer, Geoffrey F. "Now Let Our Hearts Within Us Burn," # 495.
Updike, Wayne, "With a Steadfast Faith Together Let Us Walk" # 497.

Isaac the Syrian. Quoted in Richard Foster, *Prayer: Finding the Hearts True Home* (HarperSanFrancisco, 1992), 41.

Johnson, Ben Campbell, *Hearing God's Call.* (Grand Rapids, Michigan: William B. Eerdman's Publishing Company, 2002), 38-39.

Living Before God: Defining Our Sense of Divine Presence, (Grand Rapids, Michigan: William B. Eerdman's Publishing Company, 2000), 61.

Pastoral Spirituality (Philadelphia: The Westminster Press, 1988), 52.

Jones, Rufus, *The Radiant Life* (New York: The Macmillan Company, 1951), 59.

Kelly, Thomas R. *A Testament of Devotion* (San Francisco: Harper and Row, 1941), 70.

Kidd, Sue Monk, *When the Heart Waits* (Harper San Francisco, 1990). Published in *Alive Now* (January/February, 1994), 72-73.

Kierkegaard, Soren, *Purity of Heart Is To Will One Thing,* Douglas V. Steere, Trans. (New York: Harper and Brothers Publishers, 1948), 102; 110-111.

Killinger, John, *Christ in the Seasons of Our Ministry* (Waco, Texas: Word Books, 1981), 96.

Lewis, C. S. *Surprised by Joy* (New York: Harcourt and Brace, 1956).

The Weight of Glory (Grand Rapids, Michigan: William B. Eerdmans Publishing Company, 1965).

McLaughlin, Ken, "I Long for Your Presence, O God," *The Practice of Prayer,* Carolyn Brock, ed. (Independence, Missouri: Herald Publishing House, 1999). 27.

Merton, Thomas, *Seeds of Contemplation* (New York: New Directions, 1949). 16.

Miller, Wendy J, *Jesus Our Spiritual Director* (Nashville: Upper Room Books, 2004). 28-29; 87; 87-88; 89; 101; 105.

Milton, John, *Areopagitica*; *Paradise Lost, Book 8* in *Complete Poems and Major Prose.* Merritt Y. Hughes, ed, (New York: Odyssey Press, 1957) 25; 77.

Mogabgab, John, "Editor's Introduction," *Weavings* (May/June, 1995), 33.

"Editor's Introduction," *Weavings* (January/February, 2004), 35.

A Guide to Spiritual Development (Nashville: Upper Room Books, 1996), 67.

Moon, Cleo Hanthorne, *Poetic Voices of the Restoration* (Independence, Missouri: Herald Publishing House, 1960), 72.

Mulholland, Jr. M. Robert, *Shaped by the Word: The Power of Scripture in Spiritual Formation*, (Nashville: Upper Room Books, 1985), 5-6.

Nouwen, Henri J. M. *Bread for the Journey:Thoughts for Every Day of the Year* (HarperSanFrancisco, 1997), 2-3; 64.

The Return of the Prodigal Son (New York: Image Books, Doubleday, 1994).

From Fear to Love; Lenten Reflections on the Parable of the Prodigal Son. This booklet was edited by Mark Nielson for Creative Communications for the Parish (Fenton, Missouri). The original material was drawn from a series of cassettes entitled "The Return of the Prodigal Son," (1998), 21.

Can You Drink the Cup (Notre Dame, Indiana: Ave Maria Press, 1996), 107.

O'Conner, Elizabeth, *Weavings*, (September/October, 1996), 30.

Peacock, Larry J. "Come to the Water," *Alive Now* (Nashville: May/June, 1994), 47.

Price, Phyllis, *Holy Fire* (New York: Paulist Press, 1998).
"On Hearing Handel's Messiah," 18-19.
"Prayer of the Beggar," 46.
"A Prayer of Unity," 53.
"Prayer of the Lame." 103.
Mary's Child (Manuscript in process)
"Jesus Prays," 28.
"The Temptation of Jesus," 31.

Robinson, Joseph A., "How Good, Lord, To Be Here," *The Lutheran Book of Worship #89*, 91.

Rolheiser, Ronald, *The Holy Longing: The Search for Christian Spirituality*, (New York: Doubleday, 1999). 9.

Ruch, Velma, *The Signature of God: Religion in the World's Great Literature*, (Independence, Missouri: Herald Publishing House, 1986), 75.

Summoned to Pilgrimage: The Temple as Focus of a Pilgrim People (Independence, Missouri: Herald Publishing House, 1994), 29-30; 31-32; 42; 46-47; 56; 72; 75; 77; 95; 107.

The Transforming Power of Prayer, Vol. 1. (Independence, Missouri: Herald Publishing House, 1999), 39; 40; 41; 66.

The Transforming Power of Prayer, Vol. 2.(Independence, Missouri: Herald Publishing House, 1999), 49; 54-55.

Distinguished Author Lectures, 1988-89, Velma Ruch, "My Heart Was Full," (Independence, Missouri: Herald Publishing House), 24-25; 49-50.

"The Discipline of Study," *The Order of Evangelists Training Resource* (Independence, Missouri: Temple School Center, 1995), 50.

"The Discipline of Presence," *The Order of Evangelist's Training Resource, 65; 81.*

"Sensing the Leading of My Spirit," *Herald* (September, 1995), 36; 45; 53-54.

"The Cross and the Shadow," *Herald* (April, 2004), 110.

"The Church of Burning Hearts," (unpublished), 59-60.

Sayer, George..*Jack: C. S. Lewis and His Times* (San Francisco: Harper and Row, 1988) 25.

Smith, Elbert A. "Behold the Waters How They Flow," *Poetic Voices of the Restoration* (Independence, Missouri: Herald Publishing House, 1960), 46.

Smith, Helen Bruch Pearson, "Benediction," Third Annual Community of Christ Seminary Convocation, January 9, 2005. The Temple, Independence, Missouri, 29.
Do What You Have the Power To Do (Nashville: Upper Room Books, 1992), 47.

Smith, Wallace B. "International Perspectives on the Temple," International Leadership Conference, Independence, Missouri, 1988, 49.

Snowden, Rita, *I Believe Here and Now* (Great Britain: Fount Paperbacks, 1981), 79-80

Suchocki, Marjorie Hewitt, *In God's Presence: Theological Reflections on Prayer* (St. Louis: Chalice Press, 1996), 57.

Tagore, Rabindranath, *Gitanjali* (Boston: International Pocket Library). .
"The Song I Came to Sing," 21.
"The Signet of Eternity," 24.
"Obstinate Are the Trammels," 26.

The Spiritual Formation Bible: Growing in Intimacy with God Through Scripture, NIV. (Grand Rapids, Michigan: Zondervan Publishing House, 1999), 50; 75-76.

The Temple:Ensign of Peace. Brochure. (Independence, Missouri: Herald Publishing House), 57.

Thurman, Howard, "Growing in Wisdom and Stature," "Prayer" in *Disciplines of the Spirit* (Richmond, Indiana: Friends United Press, 1977). 23-24; 40-41.

Tyree, Alan D., "Principle of Divine Revelation," *Saints Herald* 139, no. 5 (May, 1992).

Weavings: A Journal of Christian Spiritual Life (Nashville: Upper Room, 1994-2005).

Weems, Ann. "The Call of Lent," *Kneeling in Jerusalem. (*Used by permission of Westminter John Knox Press, Louisville, Kentucky. 1992), 6.

Woodruff, Jennifer Lynn, "On the Road," *Weavings* (January/February 2002), 9-10.

Wright, Wendy M. *The Vigil: Keeping Watch in the Season of Christ's Coming 17-18;*
The Rising: Living the Mysteries of Lent, Easter, and Pentecost, 7; 69; 83; 106-107.
The Time Between: Cycles and Rhythms in Ordinary Time. (Nashville: Upper Room, 1992, 1994, 1999) 26; 87.

Wuellner, Flora Slosson, *Prayer, Stress and Our Inner Wounds in Alive Now* (March/April 1998), 37-38.